VOLUME FIVE

Jesus the Redeemer

Direction for Our Times
As given to Anne,
a lay apostle

Nihil Obstat: Very Rev. John Canon Murphy, PP.

VF Imprimatur: ✠ Most Rev. Leo O'Reilly,
Bishop of Kilmore, Ireland.

The Nihil Obstat and Imprimatur are an official declaration that a book or pamphlet are free of doctrinal or moral error and that ecclesiastical permission for its publication has been granted.

VOLUME FIVE

Direction for Our Times
As given to Anne, a lay apostle

ISBN: 978-1-935566-94-6

Library of Congress Number: Applied For

Publisher: Direction for Our Times

In Ireland:
Direction for Our Times
The Hague Building
Cullies
Cavan
Co. Cavan
Ireland

In the USA:
Direction for Our Times
9000 West 81st Street
Justice, IL 60458
USA

www.directionforourtimes.org

V1213

DIOCESE OF KILMORE

Tel: 049 4331496
Fax: 049 4361796
Email: bishop@kilmorediocese.ie
Website: www.kilmorediocese.ie

Bishop's House
Cullies
Cavan
Co. Cavan

To Whom It May Concern:

Direction For Our Times (DFOT) is a religious movement founded by "Anne", a lay apostle from our diocese, who wishes to remain anonymous. The movement is in its infancy and does not as yet enjoy canonical status. I have asked a priest of the diocese, Fr.Connolly, to assist in the work of the movement and to ensure that in all its works and publications it remains firmly within the teaching and practice of the Catholic Church.

I have known "Anne", the founder of the movement, for several years. She is a Catholic in good standing in the diocese, a wife and mother of small children, and a woman of deep spirituality. From the beginning she has always been anxious that everything connected with the movement be subject to the authority of the Church. She has submitted all her writings to me and will not publish anything without my permission. She has submitted her writings to the Congregation of the Doctrine of the Faith and I have done so as well.

In so far as I am able to judge she is orthodox in her writings and teachings. Her spirituality and the spiritual path that she proposes to those who wish to accept it are in conformity with the teachings of the Church and of the great spiritual writers of the past and present.

Leo O'Reilly.

+Leo O'Reilly
Bishop of Kilmore

Date 16 June '06

Diocesan Seal

DIOCESE OF KILMORE

Tel: 049-4331496
Fax: 049-4361796
Email: bishop@kilmorediocese.ie
Website: www.kilmorediocese.ie

Bishop's House
Cullies
Cavan
Co. Cavan

2 September 2011

To Whom It May Concern:

I offer an update on the present status of Anne, a lay apostle and Direction for Our Times.

I initially granted permission for the distribution of the messages and written materials of Anne. This position remains unchanged. The writings and materials may continue to be distributed. As pointed out in my letter on the DFOT website, the permission to distribute the messages does not imply a final judgment on whether they are authentic private revelation. A final judgment on that question must await the outcome of an official Church inquiry into these matters.

Following Church protocol, I set up a diocesan commission over a year ago to inquire into the writings of Anne and to evaluate her reports of receiving messages from heaven. That work of evaluation is continuing and the outcome of it will be made public in due course.

I hope this statement is helpful in the clarification of these matters.

Yours sincerely in Christ,

Leo O'Reilly

Leo O'Reilly
Bishop of Kilmore.

October 11, 2004

Dear Friends,

I am very much impressed with the messages delivered by Anne who states that they are received from God the Father, Jesus, and the Blessed Mother. They provide material for excellent and substantial meditation for those to whom they are intended, namely to the laity, to bishops and priests; and sinners with particular difficulties. These messages should not be read hurriedly but reserved for a time when heartfelt recollection and examination can be made.

I am impressed by the complete dedication of Anne to the authority of the magisterium, to her local Bishop and especially to the Holy Father. She is a very loyal daughter of the Church.

Sincerely in Christ,

Philip M. Hannan

Archbishop Philip M. Hannan, (Ret.)
President of FOCUS Worldwide Network
Retired Archbishop of New Orleans

PMH/aac

106 Metairie Lawn Dr. • Metairie, LA 70001 • Phone(504) 840-9898 • Fax(504) 840-9818

Dr. Mark I. Miravalle, S.T.D.
Professor of Theology and Mariology, Franciscan University of Steubenville
313 High Street • Hopedale, OH 43976 • U.S.A.
740-937-2277 • mmiravalle@franciscan.edu

Without in any way seeking to anticipate the final and definitive judgment of the local bishop and of the Holy See (to which we owe our filial obedience of mind and heart), I wish to manifest my personal discernment concerning the nature of the messages received by "Anne," a Lay Apostle.

After an examination of the reported messages and an interview with the visionary herself, I personally believe that the messages received by "Anne" are of supernatural origin.

The message contents are in conformity with the faith and morals teachings of the Catholic Church's Magisterium and in no way violate orthodox Catholic doctrine. The phenomena of the precise manner of how the messages are transmitted (i.e., the locutions and visions) are consistent with the Church's historical precedence for authentic private revelation. The spiritual fruits (cf. Mt. 7:17-20) of Christian faith, conversion, love, and interior peace, based particularly upon a renewed awareness of the indwelling Christ and prayer before the Blessed Sacrament, have been significantly manifested in various parts of the world within a relatively brief time since the messages have been received and promulgated. Hence the principal criteria used by ecclesiastical commissions to investigate reported supernatural events (message, phenomena, and spiritual fruits) are, in my opinion, substantially satisfied in the case of "Anne's" experience.

The messages which speak of the coming of Jesus Christ, the "Returning King" do not refer to an imminent end of the world with Christ's final physical coming, but rather call for a spiritual receptivity to an ongoing spiritual return of Jesus Christ, a dynamic advent of Jesus which ushers in a time of extraordinary grace and peace for humanity (in ways similar to the Fatima promise for an eventual era of peace as a result of the Triumph of the Immaculate Heart of Mary, or perhaps the "new springtime" for the Church referred to by the words of the great John Paul II).

As "Anne" has received permission from her local ordinary, Bishop Leo O'Reilly, for the spreading of her messages, and has also submitted all her writings to the Congregation for the Doctrine of the Faith, I would personally encourage, (as the Church herself permits), the prayerful reading of these messages, as they have constituted an authentic spiritual benefit for a significant number of Catholic leaders throughout the world.

Mark I. Miravalle

Dr. Mark Miravalle
Professor of Theology and Mariology
Franciscan University of Steubenville
October 13, 2006

Table of Contents

Introduction

Dear Reader,

I am a wife, mother of six, and a Secular Franciscan.

At the age of twenty, I was divorced for serious reasons and with pastoral support in this decision. In my mid-twenties I was a single parent, working and bringing up a daughter. As a daily Mass communicant, I saw my faith as sustaining and had begun a journey toward unity with Jesus, through the Secular Franciscan Order or Third Order.

My sister travelled to Medjugorje and came home on fire with the Holy Spirit. After hearing of her beautiful pilgrimage, I experienced an even more profound conversion. During the following year I experienced various levels of deepened prayer, including a dream of the Blessed Mother, where she asked me if I would work for Christ. During the dream she showed me that this special spiritual work would mean I would be separated from others in the world. She actually showed me my extended family and how I would be separated from them. I told her that I did not care. I would do anything asked of me.

Shortly after, I became sick with endometriosis. I have been sick ever since, with one thing or another. My sicknesses are always the types that mystify doctors in the beginning. This is part of the cross and I mention it because so many suffer in this way. I was told by my doctor that I would never conceive children. As a single parent, this did not concern me as I assumed it was God's will. Soon after, I met a wonderful man. My first marriage had been annulled and we married and conceived five children.

Spiritually speaking, I had many experiences that included what I now know to be interior locutions. These moments were beautiful and the words still stand out firmly in my heart, but I did not get excited because I was busy offering up illnesses and exhaustion. I took it as a matter of course that Jesus had to work hard to sustain me as He had given me a lot to handle. In looking back, I see that He was preparing me to do His work. My preparation period was long, difficult and not very exciting. From the outside, I think people thought, 'That woman has bad luck.' From the inside, I saw that while my sufferings were painful and long lasting, my little family was growing in love, in size and in wisdom, in the sense that my husband and I certainly understood what was important and what was not important. Our continued crosses did that for us.

Various circumstances compelled my husband and me to move with our children far from my loved ones. I offered this up and must say it is the most difficult thing I have had to contend with. Living in exile brings many beautiful opportunities to align with Christ's will; however, you have to continually remind yourself that you are doing that. Otherwise you just feel sad. After several years in exile, I finally got the inspiration to go to Medjugorje. It was actually a gift from my husband for my fortieth birthday. I had tried to go once before, but circumstances prevented the trip and I understood it was not God's will. Finally, though, it was time and my eldest daughter and I found ourselves in front of St. James Church. It was her second trip to Medjugorje.

I did not expect or consider that I would experience anything out of the ordinary. At any rate, we had a beautiful five days. I experienced a spiritual healing on the mountain. My daughter rested and prayed. A quiet but significant thing happened to me. During my Communions, I spoke with Jesus conversationally. I thought this was beautiful, but it had happened before on occasion so I was not stunned or overcome. I remember telling others that Communions in Medjugorje were powerful. I came home, deeply grateful to Our Lady for bringing us there.

The conversations continued all that winter. At some time in the six months that followed our trip, the conversations leaked into my life and came at odd times throughout the day. Jesus began to direct me with decision and I found it more and more difficult to refuse when He asked me to do this or that. I told no one.

During this time, I also began to experience direction from the Blessed Mother. Their voices are not hard to distinguish. I do not hear them in an auditory way, but in my soul or mind. By this time I knew that something remarkable was occurring and Jesus was telling me that He had special work for me, over and above my primary vocation as wife and mother. He told me to write the messages down and that He would arrange to have them published and disseminated. Looking back, it took Him a long time to get me comfortable enough where I was willing to trust Him. I trust His voice now and will continue to do my best to serve Him, given my constant struggle with weaknesses, faults, and the pull of the world.

Please pray for me as I continue to try to serve Jesus. Please answer "yes" to Him because He so badly needs us and He is so kind. He will take you right into His heart if you let Him. I am praying for you and am so grateful to God that He has given you these words. Anyone who knows Him must fall in love with Him, such is His goodness. If you have been struggling, this is your answer. He is coming to you in a special way through these words and the graces that flow through them.

Please do not fall into the trap of thinking that He cannot possibly mean for you to reach high levels of holiness. As I say somewhere in my writings, the greatest sign of the times is Jesus having to make do with the likes of me as His secretary. I consider myself the B-team, dear friends. Join me and together we will do our little bit for Him.

Message received from Jesus immediately following my writing of the above biographical information:

You see, My child, that you and I have been together for a long time. I was working quietly in your life for years before you began this work. Anne, how I love you. You can look back through your life and see so many "yes" answers to Me. Does that not please you and make you glad? You began to say "yes" to Me long before you experienced extraordinary graces. If you had not, My dearest, I could never have given you the graces or assigned this mission to you. Do you see how important it was that you got up every day, in your ordinary life, and said "yes" to your God, despite difficulty, temptation, and hardship? You could not see the big plan as I saw it. You had to rely on your faith. Anne, I tell you today, it is still that way. You cannot see My plan, which is bigger than your human mind can accept. Please continue to rely on your faith as it brings Me such glory. Look at how much I have been able to do with you, simply because you made a quiet and humble decision for Me. Make another quiet and humble decision on this day and every day, saying, "I will serve God." Last night you served Me by bringing

comfort to a soul in pain. You decided against yourself and for Me, through your service to him. There was gladness in heaven, Anne. You are Mine. I am yours. Stay with Me, My child. Stay with Me.

The Allegiance Prayer For All Lay Apostles

Dear God in heaven, I pledge my allegiance to You. I give You my life, my work and my heart. In turn, give me the grace of obeying Your every direction to the fullest possible extent. Amen.

On the Nature of Private Revelation

When reading these messages it is always important to understand them within the context of the Church's teaching on revelation as a whole. We gain some insight into how to understand private revelation from a theological commentary on the message of Fatima written by Pope Benedict XVI when he was Prefect of the Congregation for the Doctrine of the Faith.

"Message of Fatima" provides us with valuable direction into the process of understanding private revelation and its purpose. He rightly anticipates the questions that emerge for us in its contemplation and offers guidance in the task of prudent interpretation which will honor Christ's will for us.

What is the difference between Public and private Revelation?

Cardinal Ratzinger begins by distinguishing public Revelation from private revelation and their theological status. Public Revelation in the form of the Old and New Testament is complete. *"In Christ God has said everything, that is, he has revealed himself completely, and therefore, Revelation came to an end with the fulfillment of the mystery of Christ as enunciated in the New Testament."* Revelation, God's revealing himself to man, is complete and given to us in the Gospels.

Nevertheless, he points out, referring to the Catechism of the Catholic Church that, *"...even if Revelation is complete, it has not been made fully explicit. It remains for Christian faith to gradually grasp its full significance over the course of centuries (66)"*. In this context we can understand the role of private revelation. It is part of the process of grasping, which assists in the gradual understanding, of Public Revelation. In short, it assists us in a given period of history to understand what God has already revealed to us in Christ and in how to live the Gospel during this time.

How should we respond to Revelation?

Pope Benedict speaks about how we, as followers of Christ, should respond to revelation. Public Revelation requires the assent of Catholic faith, divine faith, because in it God speaks his word to us in human words. *"Faith in God and in his word is different to any other human faith, trust or opinion."*

In relation to approved private revelations, he goes on to say, quoting Cardinal Lambertini, later Pope Benedict XIV, *"An assent of Catholic Faith is not due to revelations approved in this way; it is not even possible. These revelations seek rather an assent of human faith in keeping with the requirements of prudence, which puts them before us as probable and credible to piety."* Regarding the role of such private revelations, he says: *"Such a message can be a genuine help in understanding the Gospel and living it better at a particular moment in time; therefore it should not be disregarded. It is a help which is offered, but which one is not obliged to use."*

How should we understand prophecy?

As well as understanding its relationship to public Revelation, the nature of private revelation itself is of significance in helping us towards its prudent interpretation. Private revelation can contain elements to be understood literally or symbolically, and also both. Cardinal Ratzinger quotes Cardinal Sodano concerning visions, *"[they] do not describe photographically events in the future, but synthesize and compress against a single background facts which extend through time in an unspecified succession and duration."* Here he is articulating for us that the images and visions contained in private revelation have layers of meaning that are not necessarily bound in time and space in our human sense of them. Cardinal Ratzinger further states, *"not every element of the vision has to have a historical sense. It is the vision as a whole that matters...the center is found where the vision becomes a summons and guide to the will of God."* From this we can gain insight into both the nature of the images and their capacity to be symbolic and multifaceted, but also and more importantly, the purpose of them-"*...a summons and guide to the will of God*" and *"to help us to understand the* *signs of the times and to respond to them rightly in faith."* Further to this he states, *"Prediction of the future is of secondary importance...what is of primary importance is the declaration of God's will for the present time."*

In a recent address concerning the figurative language used by Jesus in St. Mark's Gospel, chapter 13, Pope Benedict XVI states:

"For this reason Jesus does not describe the end of the world and when he uses apocalyptic images he does not conduct himself like a "visionary." On the contrary, he wants to take away the curiosity of his disciples in every age about dates and predictions and wishes instead to give them a key to a deep, essential reading, and above all to indicate the right path to take, today and tomorrow, to enter into eternal life."

Our understandable 'curiosity' should not become a distraction from the deeply personal and meaningful contact which awaits us in the Gospels and which private revelation ushers us toward ...*"what is essential is the actualization of definitive Revelation, which concerns me at the deepest level."*

Sections of this Volume refer to the darkness which will encircle the earth and speak in terms similar to many places in Sacred Scripture using a genre of writing known as apocalyptic. It is helpful therefore to understand these writings within the context of Revelation contained in Sacred Scripture. We encourage you to read the following passages as you read this book. They are as follows: Mark 13:24-27, 32, Matthew 24:29-31, 36, Luke 21:25-28, 29-33, 2 Peter 3:10 and frequently throughout the book of Revelation.

In summary:

- God revealed Himself in divine Revelation. This Revelation is found in the Scriptures and the Tradition of the Church.

- The response that divine Revelation requires of Christians is the assent of Catholic faith, i.e. divine faith.

- Divine Revelation, which took place in Christ, is complete but it has not been made fully explicit.

- Private revelation does not add anything new to the deposit of faith. It has a role in making divine Revelation explicit. It also assists us in a given period of history in understanding what God has already revealed to us in Christ and in how to live the gospel during this time.

- Private revelations seek an assent of human

faith in keeping with the requirements of prudence, which puts them before us as probable and credible to piety.

- Private revelation is a help which is offered but which one is not obliged to use.

- Private revelation can contain elements to be understood literally or symbolically.

- In regard to visions, prediction of the future is of secondary importance. What is of primary importance is the declaration of God's will for the present time.

Part One:
Jesus the Redeemer I

May 3, 2004
Jesus

My children experience many fears with regard to their worldly existence and their physical safety. Children, at this time I would like to remind you that your body is only the temporary dwelling place of your soul. Your soul is the eternal part of you. You will not need your body for very long in comparison to how long you will exist without it. Concentrate and prepare your soul. If you were preparing to travel to a foreign land, you would prepare in many ways. You would learn some of the language, assuming that upon your arrival and after having spent time there you would perfect your grasp of that manner of speech. You would have some arrangements made for the currency used in that land if it were different from what was used in your land. You would familiarize yourself with the habits and culture of the people who lived in that land so that it would not seem strange to you and you would know at least something of what to expect. My little souls of this troubled world, this is what I am asking you to do now. When you begin to feel fear, you must think of heaven. Tell*

*Meaning your earthly body.

yourself that instead of feeling frightened, you will consider what condition your soul must be in to make the transition from earth to heaven.

First, you will need some of the language. How do we speak in heaven? We speak of love and joy. We speak of learning, of sacrifices made on earth, of the divine interconnection between the different and varied aspects of the universes. Look up to the heavens and admire My stars. Did you know that each has a purpose in its position and life span? Would you like to understand why that is the case? I won't tell you now. You will learn later. You will look at a stream in heaven and you will learn thousands of things about that stream and what is in that stream. You will learn of its origin, its destination, and everything that occurs in between. Have you ever loved and admired a river? A lake? An ocean? Would you like to experience it in a complete way? Children, this is not even the very tip of heaven. This is the very tip of the very tip of heaven and I am not finished. I am going to tell you about heaven more than I have in the past because I want you to understand that you are coming to a vast area of love and joy and wonder. There is no fear here. Offer Me your fear. Cultivate your virtues. Talk of holy souls who have gone before you, including the saints whose stories you have heard or studied. In this way you will be not only prepared for the transition, you will eagerly await the transition. You will pray, "Lord, I am ready. Take Me whenever it is My time." You will not cling to this life as a drowning man clings to a sinking boat. You will strike out in confidence for heaven in your soul and I will come and take you the rest of the way. You need not worry that you are not perfect. You need only be heading for heaven. I will finish whatever is necessary so that you are comfortable here.

No fear, little souls of the Father of all. Your Jesus will see to everything. Only hope and trust is necessary now. I love you and watch each detail of your time on earth carefully. As soon as it is time, I will come for you. I will not allow you to linger for any longer than is your allotted time because that would not be fair to you. Rest your fears and spend time thinking of heaven. There is a very good reason why none of heaven's inhabitants would choose to return to earth.

May 4, 2004
Jesus

Brothers and sisters in the world, please allow Me to fill your heart with heavenly gifts. There is no reason for you to live apart from My Kingdom. If you wish it, you can live your life on earth joined to us in heaven. You must practice living in faith, it is true, but like anything else, faith becomes a habit when you practice it, so much so that soon you do not even know you are exerting yourself. That is what I wish for you now and I am going to assist you by rewarding your tiniest acts of faith with supernatural gifts of faith. In this way you will only need a small bit to begin your union with heaven. What benefits can be gained by union with heaven? You will no longer have as many gaps in your peace. You will view all of your life as transient and valuable. Whether you suffer pain or experience joy, it will all be the same to you, as long as you are united to Me and to heaven. You will have no great preference, dearest soul, because you will detach to that degree. Can you imagine? It is possible if you trust Me and begin this practice. Souls in heaven look down upon their earthly brothers and sisters and sigh for them, because they understand what it is like to be in exile, without the divine vision and the divine knowledge. They remember that to live without certainty was a difficult thing, made more difficult when you lived in dark and difficult times. There have been many such times because mankind is drawn to sin through selfishness. These dark times, such as the one you are living in, create the most beautiful opportunities for holiness and sainthood. You look around and all seems hopeless. How challenging it is then to continue to hope and to allow My joy an avenue through which to flow into the darkness of your world. That, all by itself, is an opportunity for the holiest of acts, the most heroic deed of selflessness.

If you are My friend, you have probably suffered. Do not see this as a bad thing. View this as having treasures that await you in heaven because truly, this is the case. Your suffering, experienced in union with Me, moves the Kingdom toward God the Father. Your suffering, experienced in union with Me, purifies your soul as it detaches it from the earth, aligning it with the next world. Your suffering, experienced in union with Me, has saved many souls, despite the fact that you cannot see this yet. There is much you cannot see yet and if I were to show you everything, the merit from your suffering would be diminished profoundly. You do not want that because just as this suffering is accomplishing all of these things for others, it is increasing your reward in heaven. You perhaps cannot picture your reward. It is a difficult thing for a child in exile to imagine what his family will be preparing for him upon his arrival home. You must believe that this child will not be disappointed. The heavenly existence is so far beyond the earthly existence in terms of joy and security that you cannot understand it. I will shed a small bit of light on it for you.

May 5, 2004
Jesus

My dear earthly souls must fix their gaze on Me, much as a sailor will use the North Star to navigate his direction. If your gaze is fixed on Me, you will always be sailing toward heaven. There will be small diversions in your course, but generally you will be moving nearer. I speak now with firmness because I am certain there is no other way for you. If you take your eyes from Me for even the shortest period you will be swept away from your course, such are the winds of the world. You might say I am warning you of danger. Just as I seek to preserve you and confirm your destination and your journey to it, the enemy seeks to pull you from this course so that you will not achieve your goal of heaven. Children, for your own salvation, you must not divert anymore. I do not force souls to choose heaven. That would be coercion, not salvation. You must choose Me yourself. If you choose Me, follow Me. That is all. Very simple. Then why do we have all of these problems?

I will tell you most solemnly that most souls are choosing the side of darkness. They will deny this, speaking of silly things like secular humanism and a person's right to choose. I assure you that a human being does not have the right to choose against God. That is not one of the choices you have been allowed. So when a soul chooses against God, he chooses to follow the enemy. Again, this is simple. The father of lies draws souls but only those souls who say "yes" to the darkness. Choose Me, then follow Me. You would not choose Me and then follow a path that leads away from Me. Many are doing just that because they do not like the earthly sacrifices that come with following My course. Little ones, you will laugh at the nothings of this earth when you die in your body and are born into your eternity. If you have sacrificed your eternity or your crown in heaven for the nothings of this world, your regret and bitterness will be profound. This is not for you. You are for heaven so I want you to learn all about Me, your Redeemer, and God, My Father, and all of our saints and true servants. I want you to learn about My Church on earth. I want you to have the answers when someone asks you why you follow this carpenter's Son.

You must tell them, "Jesus is love. In heaven, there is only love. I want to go to heaven and spend eternity surrounded by joy and love." Will they laugh at you? They may. They laughed at Me so you will be in

the greatest of company. Is there another companion you would prefer to Jesus Christ? You are not alone during these times. I have many followers and they are all destined to work together. My love will flow through each one of My followers into each other. You will all be God-bearers in a special way so that you are able to sustain each other during this time of trial. Fear nothing, only serve in confidence and trust. You are on the side that will bring you to heaven.

May 6, 2004
Jesus

Hear My voice, little souls in the world. Serve Me. I have such need of laborers who serve with purity and dedication. Your all-powerful God needs you. This thought should fill you with determination to serve. My motives, now as always, originate in love. It is in love that I seek to save each and every soul. My love knows no limits and My knowledge of you also knows no limits. You were created by Me. In My eyes you are delightful. I love everything about you. I even love your weaknesses because it is through the overcoming of these weaknesses that you will achieve your place in heaven. I did not create you to sin, little one. No. I did not create you to sin.

Do I expect you to sin? Yes. I expect that you will experience your weaknesses. This does not surprise Me. What I want though, is for you to understand that such actions are sins, that these actions offend your God, and that you must adopt the proper attitude of repentance. I will not look much longer upon a world that flaunts sin in the faces of My servants and uses sin to mock good and holy souls. I will not gaze much longer upon this scene because I am going to change the landscape. Holiness and godliness will return. You may be certain of that. What I draw reference to now is the process in between what the world looks like at this moment and what is going to happen to cleanse the world so that we have our return to goodness.

Children, you will experience darkness. You are experiencing darkness now in the form of a tragic level of disobedience and rebellion. This has brought a darkness over your world that makes it difficult for Christian souls to have hope. Another darkness is coming and it will be a physical darkness. You will see it with your physical sense of sight. This has been foretold and does not surprise some of you, as I, Myself, have allowed many to understand what is in the future. Be at peace, holy souls, because this darkness and time of trial is willed by Me and I can only will what is good for My children. I will take many of you to heaven at that time and your reward will be far beyond your expectation. I will compensate you for experiencing this difficult time with the greatest and most sublime of graces during the transition from this world to the next. You see that you need not be afraid. Only if you have chosen against Me and continue to rebelliously sin should you be fearful. Repent. Do so now, today.

May 7, 2004
Jesus

The darkness swirls around My little ones and many suffer in the greatest way from fear because they are targets of the enemy. Children, hear Me. Listen to Me. Man cannot touch your soul. Your soul is your property, of divine origin, and protected by Me. I wish to keep you at a heavenly level of existence during this time so that you will not nourish fears. I felt fear also. What did I do? I prayed. My fears then left Me and I was able to walk the path of your redemption. I assure you, when you need My help, My help will be yours. When you need extraordinary graces, you shall have them. Trust Me in all. Believe in My presence in your life and you will exult, despite the difficulties you encounter. I wish to discuss these difficulties.

Before the physical darkness comes, there will be many upheavals, some from heaven, it is true, but some from the evil of man. There will come a time when many souls will be without food. There will be famine, yes, and there has been famine before. During this time though, there will be enough food, but the enemy will prevent it from being available to the people. You will expect this to happen and you will say,

"Our Lord has spoken of this time and we have nothing to fear." I will guide and direct you with great specificity when this occurs. You must be brave then and proclaim My Word with even greater zeal. You are My messengers. You carry the Light within and this Light will not be extinguished. Let your family be one who would choose to be hungry before relinquishing My Light to the enemy, for it is this that may be asked of you. You will be great saints and the great saints who have gone before you will hasten to assist you. Children of the Light, you have been marked by the very hand of the Savior. It will become more and more apparent that you bear My stamp. You will see an even greater division between the angels of Light and the souls who walk toward darkness. Do not be distressed by this because you must view all from the heavenly perspective.

It is time or I would not allow this to happen. The darkness draws too many. It must end. You will pray for it to end and many of you have prayed for it to end. This is the manner in which we will eradicate its hold over the world. It is painful for you to witness but you will be well rewarded. Praise Me in everything you see. When you see goodness maligned and persecuted,

when you see goodness labeled as evil, when you see goodness persecuted and punished, then you must thank Me because it is then the time draws nearer. You have been chosen to witness these times. Do not wish yourself anywhere else because I have selected you carefully. All is well. Your God assures you, all is well.

May 7, 2004
Jesus

My faithful ones have always suffered in the world, in some way or another. If you understand that this is a time of suffering and that your suffering is redemptive in nature, you will not anguish over the fact that you are suffering. Many of My little ones make their suffering far worse than it has to be by bemoaning that they are suffering at all. Do not say to yourself, "It is unfair and unjust that I suffer." Say to yourself always, "I will give my suffering to Jesus for the sake of the work He must do to save others." Say to yourself, "I am sinful in nature, despite my knowledge and belief in God, so any suffering I do is just, because I have sinned." Now little ones, I have forgiven you everything many times over. Many of you have difficulty understanding the depth of My forgiving nature and you confess the same sin, sometimes several times. You are forgiven and I forget your sins, but I ask you to suffer, not because you are sinful creatures. I ask you to suffer because many of the souls you work and live with every day may choose to go to hell if I do not have this suffering with which to obtain the great torrent of grace necessary to convert

them.*

There is little time. Even given the fact that earthly time and heavenly time differ, there is little time. Many of you will see these great changes. Many of you will see a shift in the earth so great that a vast area will be destroyed, never to become inhabitable again. There will be no rescue and rebuilding in this area. The damage will be complete. These souls alone must be assisted and this is only one of the events that will affect humanity in the days before the great darkness. The earth will be entombed by this great darkness but there will be survivors and they will then reclaim the earth for God.

I must tell you that heaven will be prepared to accept souls in great numbers. All in heaven will be busy, working to welcome the little ones who have suffered in the world. There will be joy, such joy, because it is always far worse to anticipate difficulty than it is to actually experience it. My little ones fear change. I understand. It is for this reason that I send these words. I want My faithful souls

*Cf. Col 1:24 'It makes me happy to suffer for you, as I am suffering now, and in my own body to do what I can to make up for all that is still to be undergone by Christ for the sake of his body, the Church' (Jerusalem Bible).

to be prepared for great change. If you are following Me, your Jesus, then you are ready. Do not hoard earthly things, little ones. This is not the time. All is Mine. Be generous with your brothers and sisters who have little. This is My wish for you and truly, it is for your benefit that I ask you to be giving. You will be so grateful later. Remain united to Me and all will be well.

May 10, 2004
Jesus

My children feel they are vulnerable, but I assure you today, souls following Me are as strong as can be. There is no reason to fear anything if you are following heaven. In situations where the world is changing, consider your greatest fear. Do you fear hunger? I was hungry, dear souls, more so than you realize. At the very least you can recall that I fasted for forty days. I know about hunger and I tell you that if you are prayerfully hungry, offering all to Me, I will lift your level of holiness and spirituality so quickly you will be overjoyed. Hunger is nothing to fear. Again, taken to its final degree, your body will lie down and cease to function and I will come for you. Now, in certain given situations where there is upheaval in nature, such as violent storms or events such as the one I described previously where your very earth begins to shift, there will be souls who will die. Does a merciful God seek to frighten His children? You know that I do not. And I am not threatening. I simply want you to understand and be prepared. When this happens, you must give thanks to Me. Trust Me and I will be there with you, relieving your fears and preparing you for the transition from earth to heaven. Your physical body cannot hold your soul for very long and you will die someday of something. You always knew this. Your soul is so beautiful, little one, that when you see it released from your body you will have no regrets that your time will have arrived. You will be joyful, please believe Me. I am Truth and incapable of deceit. I do not sow fear in My little ones. Truly, look forward to the day when I come for you.

Because I am preparing you, I must tell you of another situation that some of you will encounter. There are souls who do not follow Me, as you know, and these souls are committed followers of My enemy, who is also your enemy, and the enemy of all that is good and holy and true. These souls of darkness seek to impose on your world a God-less void. They seek to remove Me entirely from your life and the lives of each soul walking their path during this time. They will not succeed, of course, as you know, but they will try. This will be uncomfortable for some of My followers. This is nothing new and it has always been this way. My missionaries often gave their lives for just this reason. You will persevere, have no fear, but as has

happened throughout history, there will be sanctions imposed against followers of the one true God. How do I want you to experience these things? I want you to look to Me for an example. I was like a lamb and so must you be. I will direct you in everything. You will not deny Me and I will support you and reward you. Your very certainty that I exist will be the fuel that burns the fires of conversion for those who have been deceived. These are times of change but good change. Little children, do not fear the darkness because after darkness comes light. I am always with you. That never changes.

May 11, 2004
Jesus

Dear soul, conduct your self with dignity. Be calm and recollected. Be thoughtful in everything and make decisions prayerfully, always seeking My counsel. I do not want My followers to be overly excited. I do not want My followers to spread bad news in order to incite hysteria. There are changes coming, yes, but these changes are necessary and your Jesus is always looking out for the best possible environment for your soul to develop the greatest degree of holiness. I will see to every situation that you give Me control over. Be in the habit of constantly giving Me your concerns and this habit will be then so ingrained that during difficult times, the practice will come naturally.

I want good and holy souls to state their Christianity often. For example, when confronted with a situation that is not holy I would like to hear souls say to their children or companions, "This is not for us because we are Christians." And then, little souls, I would like to see you leave that situation. Do you understand what a powerful impact that would have on others particularly if each Christian began to live that way? Imagine the impact on entertainment if Christians began to act like Christians and refuse to frequent un-Christian entertainment. That, all alone, would begin a shift that would save an enormous number of souls. You must think of your children. If families and parents consistently rejected any un-Christian entertainment, children would grow with this habit and holiness would push back into your world. Children of the Light, you must begin this behavior at once. It is never too late to save even one soul and this practice will save many. Difficult times are coming, it is true. But the times coming are being directed by Me, despite evidence to the contrary. You need not have the last word on earth. You will have the last word in heaven when you become the saint I have intended you to become.

May 12, 2004
Jesus

Dear children, I am placing understanding in your hearts. I am also placing a divine calm in your souls so that you can proceed with peace in everything. There is work to be done. Souls must be brought back to My heart and it is through you, My servants, that I will do that. My mother stands ready to assist you in everything. Pray now, always. Offer every task, however humble, to Me in the spirit of prayer and it will become a divine ransom for a soul who is tumbling about in the darkness of your world. Offer Me every task and I can use each one to provide comfort and strength to a good and holy soul who is being attacked by the enemy. Are you sweeping the floor? Are you driving your car? Give those things to Me in prayer, little children. I will use them. You live for Me. Give Me everything in your life and I can perform the greatest of feats with the humblest of tasks. I have more information for you, but you have enough for this moment. Your Jesus needs souls. I need consolation now, children, from My friends who seek to help Me. At times I become disheartened, as I did in the Garden. If you feel that way, consider that your Savior is allowing you to experience

some of His sadness. Say to Me, "Jesus, I give You my sadness as a consolation for Your sadness." Dearest little ones, in this way you will be ministering to your Savior. You cannot imagine your reward for an act such as this one. I seek unity with My faithful souls. Open your heart to Me and I will dwell within you and then truly, you will bring Me to this world.

Part Two:
Greetings from Heaven I

May 14, 2004
Jesus

The Father has given permission for the saints in heaven to assist in this project. They will benefit the souls in the world with their wisdom and experience. I know My children are grateful for this gift. Give great praise and thanksgiving to the Father for this is indeed an exceptional grace.

St. Therese, the Little Flower

Greetings dear brothers and sisters. I, Therese, send you words of encouragement. I am a great advocate to you all. While on earth I made it a point to be at the Lord's disposal in everything. I awakened each day and gave Him my will so that each of my tasks could be used for heaven. You must begin to do this also. If many souls on earth begin to make this act each morning, Jesus will have many graces available for souls. Brothers and sisters, do not fear the changes to come in the world. I am in heaven and I assure you, this is where you want to live. The world is so temporary, and may I say, so difficult. We are constantly being pulled away from Jesus in the world. I tried so hard to remain united to the Divine Will, but this required heroic acts of detachment. You must be joyful, little ones. Look to me for example and for help. Look at my life. I did nothing special in worldly terms and yet our Lord has allowed me to help with thousands and thousands of souls. I want to help you. Ask me for my intercession and you will receive it. When you read the words of Jesus and Mary you must understand that Jesus and Mary mean what they say. On earth, words do not have the same commitment. Often words are thrown around with very light meaning attached. Not so in heaven, dear brothers and sisters. When Jesus speaks, He speaks the truth. When our heavenly mother makes a promise, she means to fulfill it. I am telling you to rely on their promises. If Our Lady says she will see to your needs, you can be sure that she will. If Jesus says He will direct everything, it is the Truth. Do not be afraid. Thank God for all of His graces and be His willing cooperative child in each moment of each day. I will help you.

May 17, 2004
Jesus

It is important that you, children of the earth, understand that you are not suffering alone. It is also important that you understand that you have many weapons at your disposal. One of the weapons that should be utilized is the intercession of the saints who have fought these fights before you. You see, dear children, there is nothing new in your world and these struggles you contend with have been contended with in the past. The saints have vanquished the enemy over and over. You will, also. Fear nothing, only serve.

St. John of the Cross

Greetings to all souls who long to be joined to the Savior. Do you long for unity with God? I ached with the pain of separation from Jesus. I walked the earth with a physical pain in my heart. I knew that some day He would come for me but it is difficult to understand during your earthly mission that time is passing and each day brings you closer to your final day on earth, after which, your time on earth will end. I say this to console you, dear brothers and sisters, because I know it is difficult and I know you become discouraged. When you become discouraged, you begin to question everything that you know to be true. Let me tell you of a temptation that nearly upset my journey. When I became discouraged, I had difficulty in prayer. This is common and nothing to be alarmed over. I knew this, however, I began to back away from prayer. You see, we often become attached to spiritual consolations and when they are withdrawn we incorrectly assume that our prayer is not working, that our God is not listening, or that we have fallen out of favor with Him. Instead of redoubling my efforts and thanking God for the spiritual challenge, I prayed less and less. Upon reading this you can imagine what transpired. I became more and more discouraged, Jesus became less and less able to strengthen me because I made myself unavailable to Him, and gradually I entered a crisis in faith. Would I change even one day of my life on earth? No. That is not the point. The point is that I could have done better in that regard. I did not turn away from our Jesus but I made it more difficult for myself to serve in joy. I continued to serve, of course, but added weights to the cross I carried for Christ. I want to spare you that mistake, dear souls of the earth, so I am encouraging you to be disciplined in your prayer lives. When you feel little consolation, I want you to tell yourself that this is because Jesus is treating you like a spiritual adult who does not require constant reinforcement. Your trust will propel you through your days and insure that you serve in faith. If you feel you are faltering, pray more.

Understand that when our Lord withholds consolations, He is still nourishing your soul. You simply do not experience it directly. The fruit of this nourishment will be apparent in your work and you will continue to see the Spirit flow through you. Do you understand? Others will be blessed because of your obedience, but Jesus is saving your reward for your time in heaven.

I, John, love you all. I am only one here among many who seek to assist you. When you are having trouble with your prayer life, you must ask me to help you. I will intercede for you before our God and ask that He send you fresh courage and strength. Do not fade away in your prayer, dear souls. Jesus is listening, whether you feel His presence or not. We are all listening to your prayers and if one of us can help with something, we do so. All of heaven hears your petitions so do not stop petitioning because your faith is weak on any given day. To do so would be similar to taking down the sails of your boat when you went below the deck because you cannot feel the wind below deck. That is ridiculous, is it not, to think that the wind stops blowing and sailing your boat simply because you cannot feel it on your face? You would laugh at such a sailor and correctly guess that this sailor would never reach his destination. The wind continues to blow, whether the sailor is on the deck or below the deck. In this way, his little sailboat continues to advance on the course the sailor has set.

Your souls are the same, dear brothers and sisters. Your prayers are your sails and the wind is the Spirit of your God. If you do not feel consolations in prayer, perhaps you are spending some time below the deck. It does not matter one bit because the Spirit is blowing your boat to the heavenly shore. Thank God when you do feel consolations. Thank God when you don't. In everything, praise your God. I am here, with God, and I give you my loving word that you will rejoice for every bit of service offered to Him while you served on earth. Please, ask me for help. God has given some of us great intercessory powers during this time and we are anxious to use these graces. We see each of your missions and understand how your mission will affect the Kingdom. We know more than you do. Ask us for help in every day and you will not be disappointed. Our God desires that we work together.

May 18, 2004
Jesus

I again encourage My children to read and study the lives of the saints who have gone before you. In this way you will see that you are not the first soul who has dealt with the challenges before you. You will also then feel more comfortable asking a saint to intercede for you, particularly when a certain saint has faced similar struggles.

St. Gertrude the Great

Greetings to my brothers and sisters. Jesus has allowed me to speak with you and I am grateful for the opportunity. I, along with everyone here in heaven, watch the events on your earth most carefully. I sometimes marvel at the distance between holiness and the lives souls are living. I marvel because I cannot understand how so many could be living without God. I also see the depth of the unhappiness on earth and that is quite consistent with lives being lived without God. It is very sad for us to watch. I particularly feel sorry for the small children who should be living their childhoods in joy and who feel such confusion and despair. This is not how God intended His world, as you well know.

What I want mostly to share with you is that I, Gertrude, had many spiritual struggles. You might say I struggled more than most. My nature was not suited to holiness in that I was rebellious. This was good because I was able to work hard on subduing my selfish inclinations. Why would this be good? Well, I have been given great glory here in heaven. My reward is consistent with the amount of struggling I did for God. I knew God was real and I knew God was good. After that, it all came naturally in the respect that if God is real and God is good, there can be no choice but to follow Him. Such discussions take place on your earth! I can scarcely follow all of the talk. I myself would find it very confusing and I myself would decide not to participate in so many discussions about things that ultimately do not make any difference in one's holiness or spirituality. Do not waste so much time, brothers and sisters. I look at your world and see constant talking, talking, and talking and very little loving. I did not repeat loving three times, although I wanted to, because I did not want to bore my readers, but truly, if there is one word that bears repeating aloud in your world it is love. There is so little love and that, I suppose, comes quite naturally when so few love God. You see, God, as the source of all love, puts great love into the hearts of His followers. Few are following Him, so they are not accepting the love He has to give. Poor, poor souls, so unloved. We in heaven love you all, particularly you souls who are not being loved by people on earth.

You must be brave for a little longer, dear unloved and lonely souls. You will not believe how much you will be loved here. I see your faces lit with joy and it makes me happy. Yes, I long to love you all. I am in the company of many such as this and we will make you so happy as we introduce you to the heavenly world that you will call home.

Jesus has asked me to share my thoughts with you. I have so many that I am prioritizing. I want to cry out a warning to those souls who are not following Christ. Dear little lost ones, you are heading for more unhappiness. Please take heed and serve Jesus. He is all good. You do not want to follow darkness, believe me, because it does not lead to a place where you will be happy. You will be happy here, I promise you. We will welcome you and take care of you and soon you will be so at home and happy that you will be begging to care for others. We are a family and you are part of that family. Our Father, God, wants us all home safely and we, the saints, are being allowed to help bring souls back. This time is extraordinary, yes, but you need only follow us. Ask me for help. I am Gertrude and I was far from perfect. If you feel far from perfect, I am your saint. I have great compassion for those who are struggling, as do we all. Do not be shy. Heaven and earth are joined so closely during this time that you will sometimes feel our presence. We want to help.

Be joyful as we are all joyful here and you can begin to experience that joy as you detach from the world. My brothers and sisters, I must tell you that heaven is great fun. I often hear earthly conversations about heaven and I laugh. My goodness, if it were as dreary as many think we would not be encouraging you to come. Now try very hard to follow Jesus and we will all help you.

May 19, 2004
Jesus

You see that your brothers and sisters in heaven are eager to assist you. I desire that all of you, whether in heaven or on earth, work together. You must remember also that the prayers of the souls in purgatory assist you. Do not forget those souls, dear ones, because they will then remember you and they pray ceaselessly. I want you to listen now to the words of a soul who is little known on your earth. Nevertheless, she has great intercessory powers in heaven.

St. Dymphna

Souls of the earth, I wish to help you. Too many of you are sad and discouraged. You are forgetting that you are children of God and there is a great inheritance before you. You are spending a small time, the smallest time really, laboring, and then you are to inherit this wonderful inheritance and come home. Your homeland consists of the most beautiful and vast lands and there you will spend the remainder of your time, eternity, surrounded by souls who love you. You will feel complete joy and safety, remembering that you served your God as best you could during your time on earth. You will not worry for the sins you committed while on earth. You will not even think of them. Your greatest joy will be in helping others because you will understand completely the difficulty others experience. That is how it is for me. I want to help others. I am the kind of person who is very interested in the business of my brothers and sisters and you should come to me if you feel sad or frightened. Ask me to pray for you. Jesus loves us very much and when you come to heaven you are in constant contact with Him. While I am speaking to Him I will say, "Jesus, you must help this soul with this problem. I beg you, dear Jesus, to give extra and extraordinary help to this soul." My dear brothers and sisters, we are not shy about begging Jesus and we do not stop begging until we get the answer we are looking for. In some cases it takes a little time, but that does not discourage us. We have plenty of time and plenty of persistence. If you are concerned about a soul who is struggling, come to me and ask me for help for that soul. Together, you and I will begin begging Jesus for His grace. We will not stop until you are satisfied that the soul is out of distress.

You are never asked to carry crosses alone, little brothers and sisters. That would be asking too much and I must tell you that the reason we became saints is that we were experts at letting Jesus carry our earthly crosses. In this way we could do heroic things because we did not try to do them ourselves. We simply turned them over to Jesus and cheerfully, (at times cheerfully, but

I must say that I was not always cheerful), resumed our earthly walk. Now this requires trust because only if you trust in the complete and total goodness of Jesus can you walk confidently while carrying a great cross. So you must learn to trust. I will help you. I will be the saint of trusting Jesus with heavy crosses during this time. When all looks grim and you are frightened, you must come to me and say, "Dymphna, get me more trust, quickly." I will begin working in heaven immediately. Jesus will not turn away from a request from a soul who is looking for greater trust in Him. In this way your cross will become lighter at once. And then we will work on the cross itself.

My dear brothers and sisters in this world, there is nothing we will not help you overcome. Souls think that because they sin heaven is closed to them. Nonsense. We all sinned. This is an error, dear souls. When you are in the state of grave sin you must turn to heaven at once for assistance. Turn to us, the saints, for any kind of help and you will get it. The enemy is active on your earth during this time. Jesus has decided that we, the elect of heaven, will also be active. This gives us tremendous happiness because we like nothing better than securing graces for you, the souls on earth. Call out to us often. Let it be your habit throughout the day. Heaven and earth are united during this time and we will fight every battle at your side.

May 20, 2004
St. Andrew the Apostle

I have so many things to say to you, my brothers and sisters on the earth during this time. First I would like to tell you that all attention is focused on you and the struggles you are experiencing. We in heaven are all walking this journey with you. God is making that quite clear to you, I know. It is important because your time is a time of upheaval, as was my time. A new, renewed Church will emerge on the other side of this travail. God will always triumph, of course, and it is good to remember this when you live in dark times. It is this I wish to talk about.

Because you live in dark times, you might have difficulty imagining a world where the Church leads the majority, who truly wish to serve God. Brothers and sisters, this is your destination. Despite the rockiness of the road you will travel, you will ultimately see the Church triumphant. When I walked the earth I knew that God would always triumph over evil. I was told this and I believed it with my whole heart. In my humanity, however, I experienced times when my belief nearly became submerged beneath the forces of evil that pressed in on me. When you face a situation in which all seems lost and your very faith is wavering, you must cry out to heaven. We are all there with you, awaiting your smallest request. We will spring into action, acquiring every possible grace of courage and fortitude. Do not think you must walk your path alone.

It takes great courage to fight the good fight. My life is a testament to that statement and I know what it is like to feel that your courage has been depleted. When I felt that way and thought I would succumb to moral weakness, I cried out to God in rebellion against my humanity. I begged Him to give me a small taste of the fortitude He displayed on Calvary. And do you know what happened, dear brothers and sisters? I was flooded with strength and courage. I became calm, clear-sighted, and every possible wisdom filled my being. Others marvelled at my presence. This is the result of calling on Jesus and relying on His graces, as opposed to your own capabilities. Without Him we are nothing but playthings for the enemy. Never let spiritual pride stand in the way of complete submission to the Savior.

Souls of the earth, I am your brother. I experienced great trials for the Church. Many of us here shed blood for the Church. What we are watching now is not pleasant in that this Church we sacrificed our lives for with such conviction, is barely defended. The attacks against God's Church are constant. This is always the way, of course, because the enemy roams. But never has there been such a time when the attacks strike into the very heart of God's Church with only the barest of replies, and sometimes, no reply at all. This is not moral courage, brothers and sisters.

I am Andrew and I love you all most tenderly. I am very determined to assist you and God has given me permission. You must defend your Church. I will help you. Call out to me and ask me how you should respond to a given attack. I will answer you. I will secure the necessary courage from the throne of heaven and I will fight alongside you. When you falter, I will be there. I will call out to Jesus, immediately securing additional courage and wisdom for you. I, Andrew, will defend the Church of God with you during this time. Use me. You will not be sorry you secured my help.

May 21, 2004
St. Barnabas

I, Barnabas, send my most affectionate greetings to all who search for God's will. It can be a difficult thing to be comfortable with His will because often there are sacrifices necessary. We, the souls in heaven, remember vividly the experience of having difficulty with the sacrifices we were called to make for Christ. In looking back to my time on earth, I must say though that the sacrifices I made for Him give me the greatest joy here in heaven. It is like putting something away to enjoy later, knowing that you will get one thousand times greater enjoyment from this thing if you give it away at the present time and save it for the future. I hope I am being clear about this because from what I can see of your struggles, a great many of you are having difficulty with material possessions and the wish to overeat and over drink. You have difficulty with the idea that these comforts and pleasures might be withdrawn from you. As one who had to do without those things in my service to God, I assure you, they are only a burden. You will be liberated without them. Now this is not to say you should wear no clothes and abandon your homes. I am not saying that. I am saying that you should detach yourself from the things of the world by paying less attention to them. You should eat to sustain yourself, yes, but you should not eat until food becomes bad for you. Food and drink can pull you away from God because you begin to care more for the cravings of your body than the cravings of your soul.

Try this experiment. Pray one day and eat and drink to your heart's content. Pray one day while strictly limiting your food and drink to what you require to sustain your body's functioning. On the third day compare the prayer experience of the two days. You will find, I am certain, that you experienced God more profoundly on the day you ate to sustain yourself. Brothers and sisters, this is not because you are better at prayer when you are hungry. It is because God is able to communicate with your soul more effectively when you are not sated with too much food and drink. If you care too much for the things of this world, you cannot possibly care enough for the things of the next world, where material possessions mean nothing. I speak the truth and I speak the truth to help you because I am watching the earth and those on it and I see that this is a grave hindrance to many of you.

Please heed the words of someone who has gone before you and someone who seeks to help you. We are assuring you that we want to be involved in your struggles. Let me promise you this. If you want to change your habits with regard to food, drink, or materialism, you must call out to me. I will help you. Simply ask me to obtain the graces you need and I will do so. I will be your guide to over-indulgence. If you are concerned that this might be an area for you to improve in, then we will work together. I feel only the tenderest love for you and Jesus wants to lead you and love you. The problem for you could have to do with your material concerns so we must rectify that and then Jesus can flood your soul with the greatest of spiritual graces. Call on me, souls. I am here.

May 22, 2004
St. Anne

Greetings to all souls on earth. I am grateful for the opportunity to send you words of encouragement. It is through the great mercy of God the Father that this is being allowed and you must all remember to give thanks to Him for this and for every grace He has given you.

During my time on earth, I was very aware of the graces that flowed from heaven. As the mother of the most beautiful little jewel in God's Kingdom, Mary, it was not difficult to remain aware of God's grace because great graces flowed through my little Mary even in her infancy. This is the truth. Mary, from the first, allowed God's grace to flow through her. Purity is like that.

Children of the world, you must reacquire God's purity. Purity does not seek out impure entertainment. Purity flees from such things. In your world today God's children are surrounded by filth and have become so accustomed to the presence of filth that most do not object to this constant flow. It would be helpful for your soul and the development of the virtues you need, to begin rejecting everything that is impure or suggests impurity. Certainly in some cases your entertainment will have to change, but children, in many cases, you spend far too much time with entertaining yourselves and far too little time with prayer and considering Jesus and His will for you. Sit in silence and you will walk away consoled, reconciled, and at peace. If you spend that same time in consideration of entertainment that is not suitable to be shown in heaven, then you walk away, further from Jesus, further from His will, and nearly in a trance of darkness because your mind has just spent time with someone who does not serve God.

Use this as your guide. As you view entertainment, I ask that you remember and recall that Jesus is seated with you. Is Jesus enjoying this entertainment? If not, it is not suitable for you. If not, it is not suitable for any children in your care. Parents, I was a mother and understand that parenting is a constant thing during the time of your children's formation. You must begin to forbid your children from participating in inappropriate entertainment, using the little test I have given you. Ask Jesus if a thing is suitable for your children. He will answer you. Then you must forbid it if necessary.

Parents, do not fear the anger of your children. God faces your anger every day because His children on earth continually protest that they want this thing or that thing and more of all of these things. God knows what is best for you and He is acting accordingly. He is not afraid that you will be angry. As earthly parents you have a challenge before you because in many areas of God's world, souls are comfortable with impurity in entertainment, dress, and speech. To return to purity is more difficult than to never allow these things and to have to do this alone would be very hard. That is why God has sent so much help during this time.

I, Anne, nourished and loved the most pure little human being ever created. Mary, your mother and my mother also by heavenly decree, will assist you in restoring purity to your home and family. I, myself, will also help you with this. You must call on me regularly and I will intercede for you to obtain the graces you need to determine what is impure and how to remove it from your home and your life. You must trust that I have seen everything and I do not fear the most vile examples of impurity. Call on me. I will help you. As we remove the impurity from your life, little soul, you will be filled more and more fully with the most beautiful thoughts of heaven. Your soul will settle quietly and you will feel peace. Your family will become the peaceful refuge that God intended it to be. The more you remove impurity, the more sensitive you will become to it as an affront to the Godhead. This is good because then you will all begin to object when impurity is forced upon you.

Be diligent in monitoring your manner of dress, please. If a woman dresses in a manner that suggests she is considering sin, this will encourage others to consider and contemplate sin. Please use the same test. When you are dressed, look at your clothes and say, "Would Jesus like the way I am dressed?" If not, dear little ones, you must change your clothes and put on something that will please Jesus and will announce to all that you follow Jesus.

I am Anne and I wish to help you to restore purity to your world. I have followed the progress of impurity in your world and I do not judge, because that is for God, but I beseech you to heed my words. There will be a price to pay for impurity, little children of God, and it is too high. Commensurately, there will be a great reward for those who have remained pure or rejected impurity during these times.

I may sound stern to you but that is because I am a mother and a mother is stern when she sees something dangerous, either to her own children or to the children of another. I am the most devoted servant of Mary, my earthly daughter and heavenly mother. She worries for each of you. With her, I will help you with this terribly important area of your life.

Part Three:
Jesus the Redeemer II

May 24, 2004
Jesus

I am taking this opportunity to advise My brothers and sisters about events that will come upon the world. In this way, as I have said, you will not be fearful because you will know that I have foretold these things and thus you will see that the hand of God is present.

Today I would like to talk about dissension in My one true Church. There is coming a time of even greater disobedience, when many more will turn away from My Church. This will create even more difficulties for the Holy Father, who seeks to retain unity, per My dictates. Rebellious souls often blame someone else for their disobedience and so it will be in this time. Children, many of you will see this occurring and you will see great divisions. Do not fear that you will be left without a shepherd because I am your shepherd. In the time of confusion you must remain faithful to My Church, yes, and to the leaders who remain faithful to My Vicar, whom I will have chosen. It is quite simple and you will not be misled because you will be following Me. Let others discuss, as is the way of your troubled world. You need not discuss. You need only give praise to the Father and follow the path I have set out before you. Can you understand why it is so important to convert souls before this time of great confusion? If a soul is already following Me then he has practiced remaining true to the course in the face of challenges on the journey. This spiritual experience will provide the greatest of consolations to My children during this time. I love you all so deeply and know you so well. You will have everything you require spiritually to discern when necessary.

Already My Church is struggling with a grave rebellion, which is like so many hands trying to pull it down into oblivion. This will never happen. Those attempting to do this not only rebel against My Church but against Me personally. They will be treated accordingly. If you are one who has decided that you are above My Church, and therefore above Me, take heed. You will not succeed in your effort to destroy My Church on earth and you will pay a grave price for your actions against it. Turn away from this path to damnation. Man must always be alert in order to avoid the trap of pride, which can lure a soul away from Me. Once man has embarked on this path it is difficult to divert because of the nature of this sin.

Please, if you are called upon to serve in My Church, you must serve. If you are called upon to lead, then you must lead. Pray ceaselessly, sons of God, that you may not be tested in this area. Many of you are not armed against this trap. You must adore Me in the Sacrament of the Eucharist. There I will answer all of your questions. I tell you solemnly today, any priest who leads souls away from My Church, either by his words or example, will answer fully for each and every soul.

May 25, 2004
Jesus

Little souls of the Kingdom, be alert for My guidance. You will find it in many areas of your life, but mostly, you will find My guidance in the quiet of your soul. You must spend time in silence each day. The world objects to silence, as I have told you, and will try to sabotage your attempt to achieve this quiet. You must be diligent about this, dear ones, because in order for Me to lead, you must follow. In order for you to follow, I must lead. If you are not methodically following My voice each day of your life, you are vulnerable to being misled by the winds of this world. Spend time with Me in silence so that you can hear My voice. You will never be disappointed if you are a soul who seeks My guidance. I will not abandon My own.

Now I wish to tell you about something that concerns Me. There are many who claim to be My followers. Some follow My lead, but others do not. They follow their own will, but do so behind a guise of obedience. The reason this obedience is a guise and not a genuine obedience is because they have rejected My Church in that they feel they have a greater wisdom than the soul whom I chose to represent

Me. Children of God, you are accountable. Do you think that I made a mistake when I asked this current man to be My earthly Vicar? Well then you must take that up with Me upon your entry into My Kingdom. That will be the appropriate time to discuss what you may feel are the mistakes I have made. Until that time, I am calling on you to be respectful, obedient, and supportive of this man, your Pope.

Priests, in particular, are not serving Me when they lead others to doubt the Holy Father. Souls feel that priests have a greater wisdom than others, and if a priest is following My voice, this is usually true. But priests who are following My voice are not behaving in a disobedient and disrespectful manner toward the leader of My Church, even if they do not always agree with how this man is leading. The true spirit of God does not manifest in cynicism, dear souls, so when you see cynicism, you may be assured that I am not present and I am not directing the conversation. This will increase in your world. I do not like to tell you this but I must. You must be alert always for these signs. I would like you to respond with quiet firmness in the face of cynicism.

When souls criticize My Church and its

leaders, you must direct them to Me. They should never spread disunity among My followers. If they bring their concerns to Me in prayer I will give them the light to understand exactly what is happening and why it must be. I do not abandon My Church, I assure you, and those who constantly criticize its leaders are speaking with little faith because if I allowed leaders to dismantle what Peter began for Me, it would be the same as abandoning it to a flawed humanity.

Be one who defends the Church. Let it be known that you will not tolerate My Church being ridiculed and vilified unjustly. The very priests who disobey and foster disunity are often the priests who have consistently sinned against Me. Pray for them but from now on defend My Church. I will help you and show you how I want you to respond to the attacks you witness. You must arm yourself in prayer and understand that this is a spiritual battle. I am with you and will remain with you.

May 26, 2004
Jesus

I speak to My children as the Resurrected Christ today. My wounds no longer emit the blood of My body, but remain, nevertheless. It is through these wounds that I separated you from darkness, dear souls. Do not waste this sacrifice. I would have each of you dedicate a portion of your day to My Passion, because through it you have been saved. It is the cornerstone of your faith and this is why so much of Church practice centers around this redemptive act. Children of heaven, study My Passion. You will never complete the school of the Passion because there is always more to gain from the study of it. I will infuse the greatest of graces and wisdom to those who give Me a part of their day for this purpose. You may make the Way of the Cross. You may say the Sorrowful Mysteries of the Holy Rosary. You may sit in silence and contemplate a crucifix. Or you may simply close your eyes and ask Me to accept your company. Remember that you can experience the Passion with Me daily in the sacrifice of the Mass. Children, I will never leave you. I have not left you now. Be certain that you do not leave Me.

I would like to tell you about another snare that can trip many of My followers. You must remain free from the influences of the enemy. I know this can be difficult, but not if you remain true to the direction I have given to all Christians. During this time there are many who seek guidance. This is because so many are lost and I understand that this is the case. But souls are not seeking guidance from Me, but from My enemy. They do this in the form of self-improvement strategies that seek to turn the soul into its own god. If you want to develop and grow, dearest ones, and I agree that you should do this, you must do it through the strategies I have put in place for you, and not the enemy's version of self development. Be vigilant.

Priests, you must direct souls in this serious matter. I am the Lord your God. You shall not place false gods before Me. I tell you in the most solemn manner that souls will be punished for their time spent with these playthings of the enemy. Your soul belongs to Me. You risk it in this manner and, at the very least, you give time to the study of yourself when you would benefit by studying Me. Do you want to improve, dear souls? I commend you for this. You must become more like Me. And who is like Me? My saints and followers.

Are you confused about who is following Me? Look for kindness, a quiet joy and a steady bearing toward heaven. Above all, look for someone who speaks the name of Jesus Christ in everything. That soul is following Me. There are those who speak My name but carry many grudges and spread anger and enmity. This soul is not living the Truth. I will not leave you to wonder. I will guide you in everything. But again I say to you, be vigilant and do not spend time with My enemy.

May 27, 2004
Jesus

Children of the world, I call out to you in warning. I do not desire to watch your world generate more darkness. I am allowing My angels to strike at the world in order to distract souls from their worldly pursuits and draw attention to their God. When a soul lies down to die, that soul is not concerned with the things of the world, but considers then the things of the next world. Because man has been deceived, man thinks nothing of the next world. Souls following the world have turned their attention almost exclusively inward, giving constant and total consideration to self. This, of course, will cease when man is forced to look up to the heavens because the heavens have opened, releasing warnings and punishment. I do not seek revenge, dear ones, only justice and an end to the darkness. You have been told of the coming physical darkness which will entomb the earth. Before that time you will have warnings in the form of disturbances in the sky. The moon will glow with a red color that will be easily seen. Men will attempt to explain this scientifically. You will know it is a warning. When you see this, prepare yourselves for the time of darkness because it is imminent.

To prepare you must remain recollected in prayer. Consider heaven and your transition from earth to heaven. We have spoken about this at length and you know that you need not fear. I will never leave you and I will be with you in every moment. Remain in the state of grace so that My graces flow freely to you. Be reconciled with loved ones and cast away grudges. If I desire that you prepare in practical and concrete ways, you will be told. I will see to everything.

Dear ones, I give you these words because there are those among you who will witness these events. This is a time of grace and these words are a portion of those graces that have been reserved for this time. You are benefiting from the graces obtained by souls who have gone before you. You should give thanks for these graces because through them many souls are being saved.

I also give you these warnings so that you will heed the words in this series of messages and prepare your souls accordingly. You know that you will not remain on earth forever. You have always known that. I simply wish you to be informed that you live in a grave time, a time that will know many changes. If you are following Me you will not be afraid. You will welcome the changes because you will welcome an end to the darkness. Only My true followers recognize the extent of the darkness and the extent of My disappointment and revulsion. Be at peace. Continue to pray because your prayers change the course of events on earth and many souls avoid eternal exile because of the prayers of the just. How you will be rewarded, dear followers. How you will be celebrated. If most behave in a holy way, it is easier to be holy. If most behave in an evil way, it is more difficult. Your God is grateful for each sacrifice and each decision for heaven.

May 28, 2004
Jesus

Children of the world, listen to My voice. I speak not only through these words but also directly into your soul. I speak through the mouths of prophets, but also through the graces that flow from the Consecrated Host. Listen to My voice, followers of God. I appeal to all men of good will at this time. When you listen to My words you must hear with your hearts because only then will you amend your lives and follow the Savior. I have died for you. You have been redeemed and have a right to your inheritance in heaven. Do not abdicate this right for the sake of sin. Sin holds nothing for you. When you peer into darkness, you will see nothing, because there is nothing there. When you peer into the heavens, a glorious vista will open up before you. All eternity is not long enough to explore and enjoy what you will find in the heavenly Kingdom. Look for My eyes in your soul, men of good will. Truly I ask you, which will you have? If you choose heaven, and of course you must, then you must follow Me with all abandon today. Do not wait until tomorrow because you might find that your life ends while you are still peering into the darkness. You may then find yourself committed to darkness and that is not what I want for you.

During the time when the earth experiences the physical darkness, there will be the greatest terror among those who do not know the Light. Where can they run? Behind whom will they hide? They will find that they recognize the spirits of evil because they have become familiar with those same spirits in their lives. This will not console them because the spirits of darkness are not congenial. I say no more. Those of you who know these spirits must imagine the rest for yourself. Do you think your Jesus sounds cold? Am I stern?

Souls, if you have been listening to Me with your hearts, you will know that I hold only the greatest love in My heart for each and every creature on the earth. But your Lord is not foolish and only a foolish being would ignore His enemy and the damage His enemy does to His children. I have entreated you and beseeched you to come back to Me. If you choose not to return, I leave you to your choice.

For souls who know the Light there will also be fears, of course, because this will be a time of the unknown and none can be completely prepared for such an experience. I am with each soul who knows

the Light. My grace flows into each of these souls in a continuous stream of consolation and guidance. Such will be our unity that people will communicate with Me constantly through prayer. Any person who follows Jesus Christ will be comforted. Any person who makes an act of sorrow and contrition for his sins will know Me instantaneously and be the recipient of My light and guidance. I am a God of mercy, first and foremost, but I am also a God of justice. My justice, tendered with mercy, will flow into your world. Be joyful, followers of heaven, for your prayer will be answered and your souls liberated.

May 29, 2004
Jesus

Souls of the world, take heed. Your Jesus will return. The process of My return has already begun, but there are difficult times ahead. For those of you who set your vision on the heavens, you will find the time of transition manageable. It will only bring you closer to Me. Those of you who have your vision set on the things of this world will struggle. Remember the one Truth and that is you will each die someday. Regardless of what transpires between that day and this day, you are going to face the same end. Ultimately, you will have to relinquish anything you will have acquired. All that will last are your deeds of good or evil. Cast away the things of this world. I want My children to live simply. Look for your role in the Kingdom and you will find it. I have instructed you on how to pray and how to find Me. I do not wish to frighten and if you are unduly frightened that is possibly a sign that you are fearful of losing material possessions. You must care about My will for you and completing My will for you in each day. My dear ones, your Jesus is with you now and I will be with you in every moment of your life on earth.

I am going to share another piece of information with you so that you will be able to recognize the times. When the moon glows red, after the earth shifts, there will come a false savior. He will claim to be from heaven but I solemnly assure you that I do not send this man. He will be from the enemy and a false messiah. Many will follow him simply because they do not want to suffer. You, My children, must not. You will not be confused, have no fear. Those of you listening for My voice will hear it clearly and you will know that this man leads souls away from heaven.

When you spend time with Me in prayer, you come to know Me. You know how I speak, think, and respond to the difficulties in your life. You also, equally important, know how I am not. You know how I do not speak, think, and respond. You know that I do not want power for you and if I give you power I give you great guidance to protect you from pride.

Children, take heed. This man will not speak, think, or respond to life's difficulties as I do. You know that I am not arrogant and yet this man will be arrogant. Would I send an arrogant man to lead you out of difficulty? I tell you, no. I would not. Have no fears about this.

Throughout the history of the world there have been others who have sought to lead great numbers away from Me. It will not happen. My followers are being well prepared and will withstand every test in faith and love. All is well, dear ones. You have every heavenly being to assist you in any and all of life's difficulties. I, Jesus Christ, assure you today that all will be well.

Part Four:
Greetings from Heaven II

May 31, 2004
St. Francis of Assisi

I send the most joyful of greetings to my brothers and sisters on earth. I praise God for the opportunity to speak to you during this time when so many struggle to find their direction. Jesus, who shares our humanity, understands that souls on earth need encouragement and that is why He has allowed this communication. Brothers and sisters, remain joyful in each day. I look around the heavenly Kingdom and know that you will be here with me. When I do this, my thoughts are so happy. I want to share these happy thoughts with you so that regardless of what you see when you look around on earth, you will understand what is in your future. Dearest souls, I would not be here if I did not serve Jesus during my time on earth. I do not regret one moment of service to Jesus. What I would regret, if our Lord allowed regrets in heaven, would be each moment where I failed to serve Jesus.

I want to take my time in talking to you to discuss Jesus and His great love for you. When you meet Him, you will be filled with humility and happiness. You will say, 'Of course. This is Jesus. He is why my heart was always restless on earth. I wanted to be with Him.' He is all patience and all love but you must understand that Jesus has feelings. If He did not, He would not have given humanity the ability to feel hurt and pain. Jesus longs to be loved by you as this gives Him a return on the great love He sends out to each one of us. You will understand completely when you leave your world, but I tell you that understanding is possible for you on earth if you continually offer yourself to Jesus. That is what I did. I read Scripture and said, "Lord, what is it You wish to tell me?" He answered me through the beauty of Sacred Scripture and He will answer you also in this way and through the Spirit that flows through His words. The words of Scripture come from heaven, children. Do not be misled. Jesus did not allow mistakes in those writings in that the Spirit will not mislead you. Humanity often judges Jesus by its own standards and I assure you, this is not an accurate way to judge. I am smiling as I say this because when we are still in the world, our vision is limited. Even in rapt contemplation it is difficult to grasp the enormity of the heavenly plan or the greatness and goodness of God. But we must try, mustn't we? Spend time in contemplation of heaven. Look at God's created things and give constant thanks and praise to the one who is capable of thinking up a flower! Consider the clouds, little souls. How you will soar through such clouds when you reach the heavenly Kingdom. Each cloud is a formation designed by the Heavenly Artist. Would you like to design a cloud and then watch it float across the sky? Children, this would be nothing for a heavenly soul. We are given the greatest of opportunities in heaven.

I, Francis, am the saint of heavenly joy because I allowed Jesus to let His heavenly joy flow into me while I suffered on earth. You should do this too and you will pay little attention to earthly discomforts. Can someone take the clouds from you? Not likely, unless they imprison you, and the opportunities to give God glory from a prison cell are so numerous that I cannot list them. If you are imprisoned, either in a body of sickness or in a building that contains you, you must thank Jesus because if you look at it from the heavenly perspective you will see that you have the greatest opportunity to offer Jesus your imprisonment during your time on earth. You will soar with that much more freedom when you reach the heavenly shore. I will help you learn how to free your soul so that your soul cannot be limited by either sickness or imprisonment. Nothing can take away your joy if you live your life my way, serving God through His Sacred Scripture on each and every day. I am the soul of liberated joy. Come to me if you do not feel joy in every circumstance and I will show you how it is done. I, Francis, love you all and applaud your efforts to share in the joy of Christ. I am at your disposal. Cry out to me often.

June 1, 2004
St. Joan of Arc

I send my best wishes to each and every soul on earth. We in heaven watch the events in the world because you are our brothers and sisters and you are not yet safely home. We watch with the greatest consideration for the difficulties you are encountering, particularly in this time of disobedience. Good and faithful souls, take heart from my words and from the words of my fellow triumphant ones who seek to console you and to assist you.

Your time on earth will end shortly, in that each life, regardless of its length, is but a blink in comparison to eternity. When I was on the earth I found the time moved swiftly. This was a mercy because I wanted to be with God. I had doubts, as we all did, but I wanted my earthly exile to end. You may not feel that way. You may be frightened of making the transition from earth to heaven, which is dying in your body. Many experience this fear so you are not alone. I want to tell you not to be afraid, especially if you are following the way of Jesus. I died, some would say, in a terrible way, at least as far as those on earth would consider. Let me share my experience of it so that you may know the truth.

I died with the greatest of joy. I knew Jesus was coming for me. I knew this. Did I know this because I experienced apparitions and extraordinary promises? No. I knew He was coming because He tells us He is coming. Read Scripture and take each one of His promises to your heart. He is preparing a place for you. Would He forget to collect you when He has worked to create a beautiful and perfect dwelling place in heaven for you and only you? Please, brothers and sisters, you cannot trust too much in Jesus. Such a thing would be impossible. The problem is always that you do not trust Him enough. I would love for people to be confident in Jesus because if they were, they would have no fear. I want you to trust Jesus more and more, beginning today. I, Joan, will help you to do so.

When you trust Jesus, you have no fear. When you trust Jesus, you have the greatest of confidence in your heavenly direction. When you trust Jesus, you can look at those who speak deceitfully and you can immediately detect and identify the falsehoods. Your comfort with Him is so great that you are able to represent Him in an effortless fashion. Then, when it comes time to die, you do not fear, but trust. You look around at the earth and all you have managed to do for Him and you say, "Finally, it is over. I am ready." Now, you may feel you have done little for Him. Whether you have done little or whether you have done great things, you must serve Him in earnest today.

Perhaps you are anxious to serve but do not understand what Jesus is asking of you. You should sit silently in prayer and ask Him. Then rise, and with the greatest of confidence, walk into each day. Because you have asked Him, He will reveal His will to you, enabling you to determine exactly at each given moment, what He needs from you. You may not know what He will want from you in two years, or two months, or two days, but you will know what He is asking of you today and that is all you need concern yourself about. You can hardly jump ahead to next year's tasks, now can you? Stay in your present day, where He has placed you, and serve Him.

I, Joan, want to help you to determine His will for you. When you are unsure, you must petition me. Say this, "Joan, who placed the greatest of emphasis on the will of Jesus, show Me what He is asking of me." That is all. I will rush to obtain the grace of discernment for you so that you understand what our Lord needs you to do for His Kingdom. I love you all. I admire your courage. Please remember that while I was known for great courage, I was really a fake. I, Joan, had no courage. Jesus Christ, however, filled me so full with His courage that I actually gave great amounts away to those who served with me. You can do this too. You need have nothing but willingness. Jesus will supply the rest. Come to me, brothers and sisters, and I will help you.

June 2, 2004
St. Padre Pio

Greetings from heaven, dear souls. I am Saint Padre Pio of Pretrilcina. I come to you in the greatest of peace, with love and encouragement. I have completed my earthly journey, but I do not forget my friends still struggling with the darkness of sin that flows freely through the world at this time. On the contrary, I think of you always and intercede for souls without pause. Continue to use me, dear brothers and sisters. You will find me alert always for your petitions and difficulties. During my time on earth I had the greatest of love for the will of Jesus Christ in my life. I tried to embrace His will in everything, even the smallest of things. There were times when Jesus would tell me that I was being granted a respite, and truly, I tell you, I would feel disappointment. I took the greatest of comfort to think I was suffering, both to console Jesus, and to save the souls of my fellow men who would otherwise be lost. I focused so completely on accomplishing these things that I experienced joy in suffering. This concerned me at times because I wondered if suffering could be called suffering when one enjoyed it. But let me clarify and say that I did not enjoy it in my humanity, but in my spirituality, which had been blessed with the greatest of gifts from Jesus Christ, my God and my all. He was very generous to me and that is why I achieved great things on earth in the quietness of my vocation. You should not look at my life and say, "Him? I cannot be like him." You should look at my life and say, "God is not asking me to be like him. God is asking me to be like me. What is that? How is it that God requires me to serve?" Then you must pray with your whole heart that you will say "yes" to this God who loves you most tenderly and needs you most urgently.

Why does He need you so urgently? Why does the God of all stoop to need His created ones? He does this because He is all wise and He wants to allow you to help in the salvation of many souls. He is giving you the means to obtain your heavenly glory, little soul, and in the process you will perform reparation on the earth, where great sins are being committed. This is of inestimable value to Him. Are you saying to yourself, "I don't understand what this man is talking about?" Well, truly I tell you, you have no need of a great understanding of the mind of God to serve Him, but while you are meditating and figuring it out, do not hesitate to serve. Serve now. Serve completely. I am the saint of service because I tried to say "yes" to everything and then looked around further to add more to my suffering and my sacrifices. I wanted to give more than He asked for because I loved Him so much and because I felt so painfully the lack of love He was experiencing on earth. I tried to compensate.

Again I say, you are not called to be me. You are called to be you. I will help you be the best you that is possible. To achieve this, you will need great graces. I tell you today that these graces are there for the asking. They are piled high in a pile here in heaven, just waiting for you to request them. Begin now, my friend, by requesting that I, Padre Pio, select a grace for you from your heavenly stack. I know you well, as I have watched you, along with the rest of the heavenly court, and I will choose something that I know Jesus wants you to have. It will flow into your soul and the process of becoming better will have begun. Jesus will be pleased with me and I will be pleased with you. Jesus is the one who wills these graces, do not forget. I am like the box boy who does His bidding by picking up the box of graces and delivering it you. I love my job and I love you.

I must tell you that the love of Jesus Christ is so vast that I cannot describe it to you. I am still learning about it myself. You will come to us some day and you will say, "Thank you God, that I served the little bit that I served." That is what I said. Ask me to obtain graces and I will immediately sift through your stack and find the grace you need most. I will then hold it up to Jesus and say, "Please, may I send this grace to this soul?" He will say "yes" to me because He loves me and because I worked for Him while I was on the earth. Someday, with the help of God, you will also intervene from heaven for souls on earth. Come to me and ask for my help as this pleases God. I send you my very best wishes and every heavenly blessing that is within my power to obtain.

Do not forget Mary, our heavenly mother. She is your greatest advocate during this time and loves you completely. She is the flower of heaven and joy and happiness flow before her as she walks. That is all. I am available to you and wish to help, so do not waste my offer.

June 3, 2004
St. Mary, an unknown saint

Heavenly greetings flow down upon you, dear children of the earth. I am thanking God tirelessly for this great and wonderful grace He has granted to souls. It is very unusual that He allows us to communicate with you in this way. I am Mary, and I am an unknown saint. There are many like me here in heaven. We are souls who were not called upon to lead multitudes. We were called upon to serve God in the quietness of our homes, as wives and mothers. Dear mothers, I cry out to you in warning. You must put your children first, before anything else. The world is trying to pull you from your home and away from your little ones. Please resist this because it will be difficult for your children if they do not have you as their base. In cases where you are compelled to work for the sake of your survival, then you must understand that every possible minute where you do not have to be away, you should be with your children. View activities that pull you from your home as temptations and resist these things. I tried always to put my vocation as a wife and mother before anything else. It is for this reason that I was brought so quickly into heaven and for this reason I am being allowed to communicate with you. I am a saint who will help you embrace your vocation to motherhood. Call out to me for guidance when you feel a conflict in your parenting or in your marriage and I will go before the Throne immediately and plead for the graces you require. I will share with God the difficulties that I experienced and how the world pulled at me. Truly, I will not pause until you have gained what you require to care for your husband and children. I wish to speak now to husbands.

Dear husbands and fathers, you must model yourself on St. Joseph. He is the guide for men and in heaven he has the greatest glory. He is gentle and kind and speaks only with great thought. Guard your words carefully, fathers, because you can wound the souls under your care in ways you cannot even begin to understand. You might look back at how you were perhaps wounded by your father and resolve that you will not emulate those mistakes. Consider the wonderful things your father did and resolve that you will copy those behaviors. Jesus will hold you accountable for the formation of your children. Many fathers in your world think that this is the mother's job. Dear men of God, your wife must have a partner in this endeavor or she will become overburdened and discouraged. Whenever possible, you must shoulder your share of this task. You will do little that is more important than the formation of your children. Jesus needs beautiful committed Christians to take up His cause and He is counting on you to bring them up. With that said, you must never think that you are alone in the formation of your children. Be humble and let your heavenly friends lead you in your parenting. I had many children and I loved each one dearly. When the children came, I had to put aside my personal wishes and desires and see to their needs. Did I become bitter and resentful? No, I did not. I understood that my children needed my attention and that the time for me to pursue outside interests was necessarily limited. I do not suggest that mothers should not care for themselves and you know that you must do this, of course. I am suggesting that in this time Jesus finds many situations where there is nobody parenting the children He is sending. He wishes this to change and I know that you will all respond to Him. Call on me for guidance in all that involves your precious families and I will help you.

June 4, 2004
St. Philomena

Greetings to all of my friends on earth. I consider everyone on the earth my friend because we are all children of the Creator. We are in the family of God together and family members must help each other in everything. I want to help you, dear brothers and sisters.

I am Philomena and I suffered for the faith. I understand what it is to suffer and I understand the temptation to comply with the desires of the world in order to escape notice and persecution. But that is not the way for us. As soldiers of Christ we must never fear the battle with the world. We will be noticed for our faith and I assure you, fellow suffering souls, that when you arrive in heaven you will be celebrated for any sacrifices you made in the name of Jesus Christ.

You live in a time of uprising, so you must rise up. Look up to Jesus and say, "Jesus, notice me. I am here awaiting Your every request. I will carry heaven's flag for a stretch." Your offer will not go by the wayside because Jesus needs those who follow Him to do their share.

Never fear the enemy's reaction. The enemy blows hard at you when you serve Jesus but ultimately the enemy has no power. You must let the winds of evil blow, knowing that good will always come out ahead.

You see that I am speaking in terms of a battle. I do that, brothers and sisters, because there is a battle being fought for souls, on the earth, but also from heaven. You think of us as being remotely located but that is not so at all. We are not limited by space so we can be with you. We can see you anywhere, even though you cannot see us. Our presence is apparent to each other, of course, so you must crowd your area with heavenly personages. We will have the gayest time protecting you if there are many of us. Call on us often and call on us all.

Often you have a problem and you will think of a saint. Pay attention to those prompts. Often a saint wants to help a soul with a particular problem so that saint will introduce herself or himself to the soul. We do this in many creative ways, such as leaving cards for you, sending you books, or generally putting you somewhere where you can spot us. Say, "Hello, dear saint, it is nice to meet you. How can you assist me?" We will tell you, despite the necessary limitations in our communication. Because earthly souls often limit us by their limited faith, I will clarify. We are with you. You do not see us but that is because you are still in your earthly state. You will see us if you follow God. That is certain. We can assist you. God allows us to share in His power as a reward for our service to Him. We want to help you and are committed to your cause. You must talk to us and ask us.

Let your relationship with your heavenly friends be as apparent in your life as your relationship with your earthly friends. This is realistic for you because we will help you to grow in your relationship with God and as you grow in your relationship with God, you will think in terms of the heavenly world that is joined to your world.

It is like you are all sleepwalkers when you do not pay attention to Jesus and Mary, to the angels, or to us saints. We stand in front of you and shout, saying, "LISTEN. WE ARE HERE." But you walk past us, thinking sadly that nobody is listening to your prayers. I am teasing you now so do not be offended but laugh with me. Truly, you must have that bit of faith and you must learn to trust us. We will never let you down. Sometimes you ask us for help with something and Jesus says that your request would pull you from His divine will. In that case we try to let you down as gently as possible, often compensating you with some other grace or joy. We love you so much and take such joy in your spiritual accomplishments. We are always trying to pull you further up the hill that is the path to heaven. The closer you get, the more we can manifest ourselves to you. Begin now, dear souls. Look to heaven, tell God you are ready to begin your journey in earnest, and say, "Philomena, come and pull me up the hill." I will be there and together we will proceed.

June 5, 2004
St. Thomas the Apostle

Greetings to the followers of the Lord Jesus Christ. I, also, am a follower, but my time on earth is completed. Because of that I have the benefit of hindsight. I suspect that many of you are guessing that I will talk about faith. You are correct. I had the greatest of faith on earth, truly, but when you live on earth, and you are following Jesus, there are times when you are asked to believe what is inconceivable to the limitations of human thinking. It is at that time that you must turn joyfully to heaven and say, "Jesus, I trust in you, I believe in you, and I will follow you." Those simple words should be said all the day long. There will come times when you will feel your faith wavering. This is perfectly normal, dear followers. You may expect to confront doubts at some time during your service. This should not affect your service in any way. Say those words and cry out to me, Thomas, and I will console you and comfort you while I simultaneously turn to the Throne and pray, interceding for you until the time of challenge has passed.

I loved Jesus dearly. He was the most tender, kind, and considerate man, as you perhaps have seen through your reading of Scripture. His eyes reflected all that is holy. People looked at Him on the road as they passed by because they knew He was special. He carried Himself with the greatest of dignity. I must tell you that once you were near Jesus, you could not bear to be away from Him. During your time of separation, you would think constantly about your reconciliation with Him and about what you would share with Him when you were back in His presence. He was everything to us.

Now imagine how we felt when He was crucified. Not only was He gone, but in such a way! We were literally sick. I tell you honestly that it was the most tragic thing I ever confronted during my time on earth. I was bereft. Then He rose. Well, when something dreadful occurs in your life, you often think in denial and say, "Maybe it did not happen." You know that it did, of course, but there is a part of you who would like to believe that it did not happen. I am a practical man and you will find that when you meet me. That is why my first task was to give you a practical practice, such as saying those words. But when a practical man is confronted with a mystical event, such as the Resurrection, his whole being is challenged. Some of you may be like that right now.

Perhaps you are good Christians but you do not understand private revelations. You might wonder how Jesus would trust such an important task to a human. I smile when I remind you that we were human also and He entrusted us with the inception and development of the early Church. That was a big job. When I did believe that Jesus had risen from the dead, I never doubted anything mystical again. How could I when I had seen what this God of ours could do? You may not believe this, dear fellow servant, but I was known for my unshakable faith.

I am the saint who will help you with your doubts. You must call on me often, as often as you have doubts, and I will rush to you because I understand the pain and anguish of wanting to serve but struggling to believe. You must understand how much I love you. Believe, dear soul, that your times are changing. This is a mercy and you should thank heaven for it. You are being well prepared and this opportunity for enhanced unity between earth and heaven is part of that mercy. We are with you at every moment. You have many friends in heaven. Use them.

I, Thomas, pledge to walk with you in times of doubt so that your service to the Kingdom is unaffected. In that situation, you gain the most powerful of graces and rewards because it is far more difficult to serve when you are struggling. What you must concentrate on always is service. I will serve! That is your refrain. God can do great things with a soul who speaks that way all day.

Now, your brother in Christ, Thomas, has given you advice. I also send you grace from heaven and as you read these words I am asking Jesus to strengthen your faith. I have already interceded for you. Call on me often and I will help you.

Appendix

The Lay Apostolate of Jesus Christ the Returning King

We seek to be united to Jesus in our daily work, and through our vocations, in order to obtain graces for the conversion of sinners. Through our cooperation with the Holy Spirit, we will allow Jesus to flow through us to the world, bringing His light. We do this in union with Mary, our Blessed Mother, with the Communion of Saints, with all of God's holy angels, and with our fellow lay apostles in the world.

Guidelines for Lay Apostles

As lay apostles of Jesus Christ the Returning King, we agree to perform our basic obligations as practicing Catholics. Additionally, we will adopt the following spiritual practices, as best we can:

1. **Allegiance Prayer** and **Morning Offering**, plus a brief prayer for the Holy Father
2. **Eucharistic Adoration**, one hour per week
3. **Prayer Group Participation**, monthly, at which we pray the Luminous Mysteries of the Holy Rosary and read the Monthly Message
4. **Monthly Confession**
5. Further, we will follow the example of Jesus Christ as set out in the Holy Scripture, treating all others with His patience and kindness.

Allegiance Prayer

Dear God in Heaven, I pledge my allegiance to You. I give You my life, my work and my heart. In turn, give me the grace of obeying Your every direction to the fullest possible extent. Amen.

Morning Offering

O Jesus, through the Immaculate Heart of Mary, I offer You the prayers, works, joys and sufferings of this day, for all the intentions of Your Sacred Heart, in union with the Holy Sacrifice of the Mass throughout the world, in reparation for my sins, and for the intentions of the Holy Father. Amen.

Prayer for the Holy Father

Blessed Mary, Mother of Jesus, protect our Holy Father, Benedict XVI, and bless his intentions.

Five Luminous Mysteries

1. The Baptism of Jesus
2. The Wedding at Cana
3. The Proclamation of the Kingdom of God
4. The Transfiguration
5. The Institution of the Eucharist

Promise from Jesus to His Lay Apostles

May 12, 2005

Your message to souls remains constant. Welcome each soul to the rescue mission. You may assure each lay apostle that just as they concern themselves with My interests, I will concern Myself with theirs. They will be placed in My Sacred Heart and I will defend and protect them. I will also pursue complete conversion of each of their loved ones. So you see, the souls who serve in this rescue mission as My beloved lay apostles will know peace. The world cannot make this promise as only Heaven can bestow peace on a soul. This is truly Heaven's mission and I call every one of Heaven's children to assist Me. You will be well rewarded, My dear ones.

Prayers taken from The Volumes

Prayers to God the Father

"What can I do for my Father in Heaven?"

"I trust You, God. I offer You my pain in the spirit of acceptance and I will serve You in every circumstance."

"God my Father in Heaven, You are all mercy. You love me and see my every sin. God, I call on You now as the Merciful Father. Forgive my every sin. Wash away the stains on my soul so that I may once again rest in complete innocence. I trust You, Father in Heaven. I rely on You. I thank You. Amen."

"God my Father, calm my spirit and direct my path."

"God, I have made mistakes. I am sorry. I am Your child, though, and seek to be united to You."

"I believe in God. I believe Jesus is calling me. I believe my Blessed Mother has requested my help. Therefore I am going to pray on this day and every day."

"God my Father, help me to understand."

Prayers to Jesus

"Jesus, I give You my day."

"Jesus, how do You want to use me on this day? You have a willing servant in me, Jesus. Allow me to work for the Kingdom."

"Lord, what can I do today to prepare for Your coming? Direct me, Lord, and I will see to Your wishes."

"Lord, help me."

"Jesus, love me."

Prayers to the Angels

"Angels from Heaven, direct my path."

"Dearest angel guardian, I desire to serve Jesus by remaining at peace. Please obtain for me the graces necessary to maintain His divine peace in my heart."

Prayers for a Struggling Soul

"Jesus, what do You think of all this? Jesus, what do You want me to do for this soul? Jesus, show me how to bring You into this situation."

"Angel guardian, thank you for your constant vigil over this soul. Saints in Heaven, please assist this dear angel."

Prayers for Children

"God in Heaven, You are the Creator of all things. Please send Your graces down upon our world."

"Jesus, I love You."

"Jesus, I trust in You. Jesus, I trust in You. Jesus, I trust in You."

"Jesus, I offer You my day."

"Mother Mary, help me to be good."

How to Recite the Chaplet of Divine Mercy

The Chaplet of Mercy is recited using ordinary Rosary beads of five decades. The Chaplet is preceded by two opening prayers from the *Diary* of Saint Faustina and followed by a closing prayer.

1. Make the Sign of the Cross

In the name of the Father, and of the Son, and of the Holy Spirit. Amen.

2. Optional Opening Prayers

You expired, Jesus, but the source of life gushed forth for souls, and the ocean of mercy opened up for the whole world. O Fount of Life, unfathomable Divine Mercy, envelop the whole world and empty Yourself out upon us.

O Blood and Water, which gushed forth from the Heart of Jesus as a fountain of mercy for us, I trust in You!

3. Our Father

Our Father, who art in Heaven, hallowed be Thy name. Thy Kingdom come. Thy will be done on earth as it is in Heaven. Give us this day our daily bread. And forgive us our trespasses, as we forgive those who trespass against us. And lead us not into temptation, but deliver us from evil. Amen.

4. Hail Mary

Hail Mary, full of grace, the Lord is with thee. Blessed art thou among women, and blessed is the fruit of thy womb, Jesus. Holy Mary, Mother of God, pray for us sinners, now and at the hour of our death. Amen.

5. The Apostles' Creed

I believe in God, the Father Almighty, Creator of Heaven and earth. I believe in Jesus Christ, His only Son, our Lord. He was conceived by the power of the Holy Spirit and born of the Virgin Mary. He suffered under Pontius Pilate, was crucified, died, and was buried. He descended to the dead. On the third day He rose again. He ascended into Heaven, and is seated at the right hand of the Father. He will come again to judge the living and the dead. I believe in the Holy Spirit, the holy Catholic Church, the Communion of Saints, the forgiveness of sins, the resurrection of the body, and life everlasting. Amen.

6. The Eternal Father

Eternal Father, I offer You the Body and Blood, Soul and Divinity of Your dearly beloved Son, our Lord, Jesus Christ, in atonement for our sins and those of the whole world.

7. On the Ten Small Beads of Each Decade

For the sake of His Sorrowful Passion, have mercy on us and on the whole world.

8. Repeat for the remaining decades

Saying the "Eternal Father" (6) on the "Our Father" bead and then 10 "For the sake of His Sorrowful Passion" (7) on the following "Hail Mary" beads.

9. Conclude with Holy God

Holy God, Holy Mighty One, Holy Immortal One, have mercy on us and on the whole world.

10. Optional Closing Prayer

Eternal God, in whom mercy is endless and the treasury of compassion inexhaustible, look kindly upon us and increase Your mercy in us, that in difficult moments we might not despair nor become despondent, but with great confidence submit ourselves to Your holy will, which is Love and Mercy itself.

To learn more about the image of The Divine Mercy, the Chaplet of Divine Mercy and the series of revelations given to St. Faustina Kowalska please contact:

Marians of the Immaculate Conception
Stockbridge, Massachusetts 01263
Telephone 800-462-7426
www.marian.org

How to Pray the Rosary

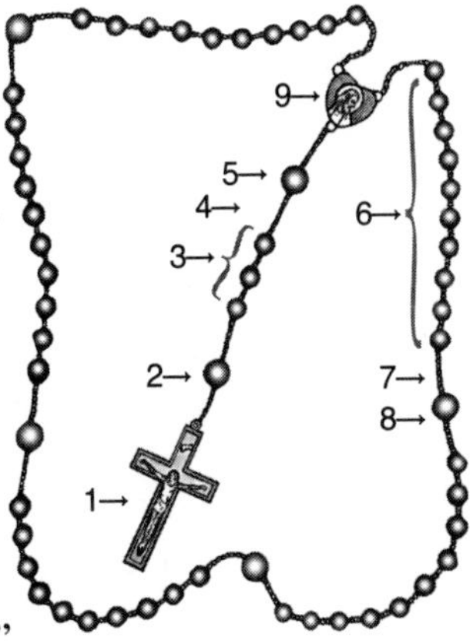

1. Make the Sign of the Cross and say the "Apostles Creed."
2. Say the "Our Father."
3. Say three "Hail Marys."
4. Say the "Glory be to the Father."
5. Announce the First Mystery; then say the "Our Father."
6. Say ten "Hail Marys," while meditating on the Mystery.
7. Say the "Glory be to the Father." After each decade say the following prayer requested by the Blessed Virgin Mary at Fatima: "O my Jesus, forgive us our sins, save us from the fires of hell, lead all souls to Heaven, especially those in most need of Thy mercy."
8. Announce the Second Mystery: then say the "Our Father." Repeat 6 and 7 and continue with the Third, Fourth, and Fifth Mysteries in the same manner.
9. Say the "Hail, Holy Queen" on the medal after the five decades are completed.

As a general rule, depending on the season, the Joyful Mysteries are said on Monday and Saturday; the Sorrowful Mysteries on Tuesday and Friday;

the Glorious Mysteries on Wednesday and Sunday; and the Luminous Mysteries on Thursday.

Papal Reflections of the Mysteries

The Joyful Mysteries

The Joyful Mysteries are marked by the joy radiating from the event of the Incarnation. This is clear from the very first mystery, the Annunciation, where Gabriel's greeting to the Virgin of Nazareth is linked to an invitation to messianic joy: "Rejoice, Mary." The whole of salvation... had led up to this greeting. (Prayed on Mondays and Saturdays, and optional on Sundays during Advent and the Christmas Season.)

The Luminous Mysteries

Moving on from the infancy and the hidden life in Nazareth to the public life of Jesus, our contemplation brings us to those mysteries which may be called in a special way "Mysteries of Light." Certainly, the whole mystery of Christ is a mystery of light. He is the "Light of the world" (John 8:12). Yet this truth emerges in a special way during the years of His public life. (Prayed on Thursdays.)

The Sorrowful Mysteries

The Gospels give great prominence to the Sorrowful Mysteries of Christ. From the beginning, Christian piety, especially during the Lenten devotion of the Way of the Cross, has focused on the individual moments of the Passion, realizing that here is found the culmination of the revelation of God's love and the source of our salvation. (Prayed on Tuesdays and Fridays, and optional on Sundays during Lent.)

The Glorious Mysteries

"The contemplation of Christ's face cannot stop at the image of the Crucified One. He is the Risen One!" The Rosary has always expressed this knowledge born of faith and invited the believer to pass beyond the darkness of the Passion in order to gaze upon Christ's glory in the Resurrection and Ascension… Mary herself would be raised to that same glory in the Assumption. (Prayed on Wednesdays and Sundays.)

From the *Apostolic Letter The Rosary of the Virgin Mary*, Pope John Paul II, Oct. 16, 2002.

Prayers of the Rosary

The Sign of the Cross

In the name of the Father, and of the Son, and of the Holy Spirit. Amen.

The Apostles' Creed

I believe in God, the Father Almighty, Creator of Heaven and earth. I believe in Jesus Christ, His only Son, our Lord. He was conceived by the power of the Holy Spirit and born of the Virgin Mary. He suffered under Pontius Pilate, was crucified, died, and was buried. He descended to the dead. On the third day He rose again. He ascended into Heaven, and is seated at the right hand of the Father. He will come again to judge the living and the dead. I believe in the Holy Spirit, the holy Catholic Church, the Communion of Saints, the forgiveness of sins, the resurrection of the body, and life everlasting. Amen.

Our Father

Our Father, who art in Heaven, hallowed be Thy name. Thy Kingdom come. Thy will be done on earth as it is in Heaven. Give us this day our daily bread. And forgive us our trespasses, as we forgive those who trespass against us. And lead us not into temptation, but deliver us from evil. Amen.

Hail Mary

Hail Mary, full of grace, the Lord is with thee. Blessed art thou among women, and blessed is the fruit of thy womb, Jesus. Holy Mary, Mother of God, pray for us sinners, now and at the hour of our death. Amen.

Glory Be to the Father

Glory be to the Father, and to the Son, and to the Holy Spirit. As it was in the beginning, is now, and ever shall be, world without end. Amen.

Hail Holy Queen

Hail, Holy Queen, Mother of Mercy, our life, our sweetness and our hope. To thee do we cry, poor banished children of Eve. To thee do we send up our sighs, mourning and weeping in this valley of tears. Turn then, most gracious Advocate, thine eyes of mercy towards us. And after this, our exile, show unto us the blessed fruit of thy womb, Jesus. O clement, O loving, O sweet Virgin Mary!

Pray for us, O Holy Mother of God.
That we may be made worthy of the promises of Christ.

The Mysteries

First Joyful Mystery:
The Annunciation

And when the angel had come to her, he said, "Hail, full of grace, the Lord is with thee. Blessed art thou among women." (*Luke* 1:28)

One *Our Father*, Ten *Hail Marys*,
One *Glory Be*, etc.

Fruit of the Mystery: ***Humility***

Second Joyful Mystery:
The Visitation

Elizabeth was filled with the Holy Spirit and cried out in a loud voice: "Blest are you among women and blest is the fruit of your womb."(*Luke* 1:41-42)

One *Our Father*, Ten *Hail Marys*,
One *Glory Be*, etc.

Fruit of the Mystery: ***Love of Neighbor***

Third Joyful Mystery:
The Birth of Jesus

She gave birth to her first-born Son and wrapped Him in swaddling clothes and laid Him in a manger, because there was no room for them in the place where travelers lodged. (*Luke* 2:7)

One *Our Father*, Ten *Hail Marys*,
One *Glory Be*, etc.

Fruit of the Mystery: ***Poverty***

Fourth Joyful Mystery: The Presentation

When the day came to purify them according to the law of Moses, the couple brought Him up to Jerusalem so that He could be presented to the Lord, for it is written in the law of the Lord, "Every first-born male shall be consecrated to the Lord."

(*Luke* 2:22-23)

One *Our Father*, Ten *Hail Marys*,
One *Glory Be*, etc.

Fruit of the Mystery: ***Obedience***

Fifth Joyful Mystery: The Finding of the Child Jesus in the Temple

On the third day they came upon Him in the temple sitting in the midst of the teachers, listening to them and asking them questions. (*Luke* 2:46)

One *Our Father*, Ten *Hail Marys*,
One *Glory Be*, etc.

Fruit of the Mystery: ***Joy in Finding Jesus***

First Luminous Mystery: The Baptism of Jesus

And when Jesus was baptized… the heavens were opened and He saw the Spirit of God descending like a dove, and alighting on Him, and lo, a voice from heaven, saying "this is My beloved Son," with whom I am well pleased." (*Matthew* 3:16-17)

One *Our Father*, Ten *Hail Marys*,
One *Glory Be*, etc.

Fruit of the Mystery: ***Openness to the Holy Spirit***

Second Luminous Mystery: The Wedding at Cana

His mother said to the servants, "Do whatever He tells you."… Jesus said to them, "Fill the jars with water." And they filled them up to the brim.

(*John* 2:5-7)

One *Our Father*, Ten *Hail Marys*,
One *Glory Be*, etc.

Fruit of the Mystery: ***To Jesus through Mary***

Third Luminous Mystery: The Proclamation of the Kingdom of God

"And preach as you go, saying, 'The kingdom of heaven is at hand.' Heal the sick, raise the dead, cleanse lepers, cast out demons. You received without pay, give without pay." (*Matthew* 10:7-8)

One *Our Father*, Ten *Hail Marys*,
One *Glory Be*, etc.

Fruit of the Mystery: ***Repentance and Trust in God***

Fourth Luminous Mystery: The Transfiguration

And as He was praying, the appearance of His countenance was altered and His raiment become dazzling white. And a voice came out of the cloud saying, "This is My Son, My chosen; listen to Him!

(*Luke* 9:29, 35)

One *Our Father*, Ten *Hail Marys*,
One *Glory Be*, etc.

Fruit of the Mystery: ***Desire for Holiness***

Fifth Luminous Mystery: The Institution of the Eucharist

And He took bread, and when He had given thanks He broke it and gave it to them, saying, "This is My body which is given for you."... And likewise the cup after supper, saying, "This cup which is poured out for you is the new covenant in My blood."

(*Luke* 22:19-20)

One *Our Father*, Ten *Hail Marys*,
One *Glory Be*, etc.

Fruit of the Mystery: ***Adoration***

First Sorrowful Mystery: The Agony in the Garden

In His anguish He prayed with all the greater intensity, and His sweat became like drops of blood falling to the ground. Then He rose from prayer and came to His disciples, only to find them asleep, exhausted with grief. (*Luke* 22:44-45)

One *Our Father*, Ten *Hail Marys*,
One *Glory Be*, etc.

Fruit of the Mystery: ***Sorrow for Sin***

Second Sorrowful Mystery: The Scourging at the Pillar

Pilate's next move was to take Jesus and have Him scourged. (*John* 19:1)

One *Our Father*, Ten *Hail Marys*,
One *Glory Be*, etc.

Fruit of the Mystery: ***Purity***

Third Sorrowful Mystery: The Crowning with Thorns

They stripped off His clothes and wrapped Him in a scarlet military cloak. Weaving a crown out of thorns they fixed it on His head, and stuck a reed in His right hand... (*Matthew* 27:28-29)

One *Our Father*, Ten *Hail Marys*,
One *Glory Be*, etc.

Fruit of the Mystery: ***Courage***

Fourth Sorrowful Mystery: The Carrying of the Cross

... carrying the cross by Himself, He went out to what is called the Place of the Skull (in Hebrew, Golgotha). (*John* 19:17)

One *Our Father*, Ten *Hail Marys*,
One *Glory Be*, etc.

Fruit of the Mystery: ***Patience***

Fifth Sorrowful Mystery: The Crucifixion

Jesus uttered a loud cry and said, "Father, into Your hands I commend My spirit." After He said this, He expired. (*Luke* 23:46)

One *Our Father*, Ten *Hail Marys*,
One *Glory Be*, etc.

Fruit of the Mystery: ***Perseverance***

First Glorious Mystery: The Resurrection

You need not be amazed! You are looking for Jesus of Nazareth, the one who was crucified. He has been raised up; He is not here. See the place where they laid Him." (*Mark* 16:6)

One *Our Father*, Ten *Hail Marys*,
One *Glory Be*, etc.

Fruit of the Mystery: ***Faith***

Second Glorious Mystery: The Ascension

Then, after speaking to them, the Lord Jesus was taken up into Heaven and took His seat at God's right hand. (*Mark* 16:19)

One *Our Father*, Ten *Hail Marys*,
One *Glory Be*, etc.

Fruit of the Mystery: ***Hope***

Third Glorious Mystery: The Descent of the Holy Spirit

All were filled with the Holy Spirit. They began to express themselves in foreign tongues and make bold proclamation as the Spirit prompted them. (*Acts* 2:4)

One *Our Father*, Ten *Hail Marys*,
One *Glory Be*, etc.

Fruit of the Mystery: ***Love of God***

Fourth Glorious Mystery: The Assumption

You are the glory of Jerusalem… you are the splendid boast of our people… God is pleased with what you have wrought. May you be blessed by the Lord Almighty forever and ever.

(*Judith* 15:9-10)

One *Our Father*, Ten *Hail Marys*,
One *Glory Be*, etc.

Fruit of the Mystery: ***Grace of a Happy Death***

Fifth Glorious Mystery: The Coronation

A great sign appeared in the sky, a woman clothed with the sun, with the moon under her feet, and on her head a crown of twelve stars. (*Revelation* 12:1)

One *Our Father*, Ten *Hail Marys*,
One *Glory Be*, etc.

Fruit of the Mystery: ***Trust in Mary's Intercession***

This book is part of a non-profit mission. Our Lord has requested that we spread these words internationally. Please help us.

In Ireland:
Direction For Our Times
The Hague Building
Cullies
Cavan
County Cavan

+353-(0)49-437-3040
contactus@dfot.ie

Registered Charity CHY17298

In the USA:
Direction For Our Times
9000 West 81st Street
Justice, Illinois 60458

708-496-9300
contactus@directionforourtimes.org

A 501(c)(3) Organization

Monthly Messages

For seven years Jesus gave Anne a message for the world on the first day of every month. Each month the apostolate reads one of these monthly messages. To receive the monthly messages you may access our website at **www.directionforourtimes.org** or call us at one of our offices to be placed on our mailing list.

We have also printed a book which contains all of the monthly messages. It can be purchased through our website as well.

The Volumes

Direction for Our Times
as given to Anne, a lay apostle

Volume One:	***Thoughts on Spirituality***
Volume Two:	***Conversations with the Eucharistic Heart of Jesus***
Volume Three:	***God the Father Speaks to His Children*** ***The Blessed Mother Speaks to Her Bishops and Priests***
Volume Four:	***Jesus the King*** ***Heaven Speaks to Priests*** ***Jesus Speaks to Sinners***
Volume Five:	***Jesus the Redeemer***
Volume Six:	***Heaven Speaks to Families***
Volume Seven:	***Greetings from Heaven***
Volume Eight:	***Resting in the Heart of the Savior***
Volume Nine:	***Angels***
Volume Ten:	***Jesus Speaks to His Apostles***

The Volumes are now available in PDF format for free download and printing from our website: www.directionforourtimes.org.
We encourage everyone to print and distribute them.

The Volumes are also available at your local bookstore.

The "Heaven Speaks" Booklets

Direction for Our Times
as given to Anne, a lay apostle

The following booklets are available individually from Direction for Our Times:

Heaven Speaks About Abortion
Heaven Speaks About Addictions
Heaven Speaks to Victims of Clerical Abuse
Heaven Speaks to Consecrated Souls
Heaven Speaks About Depression
Heaven Speaks About Divorce
Heaven Speaks to Prisoners
Heaven Speaks to Soldiers
Heaven Speaks About Stress
Heaven Speaks to Young Adults

Heaven Speaks to Those Away from the Church
Heaven Speaks to Those Considering Suicide
Heaven Speaks to Those Who Do Not Know Jesus
Heaven Speaks to Those Who Are Dying
Heaven Speaks to Those Who Experience Tragedy
Heaven Speaks to Those Who Fear Purgatory
Heaven Speaks to Those Who Have Rejected God
Heaven Speaks to Those Who Struggle to Forgive
Heaven Speaks to Those Who Suffer from Financial Need
Heaven Speaks to Parents Who Worry About Their Children's Salvation

All twenty of the "Heaven Speaks" booklets are now available in PDF format for free download and printing from our website www.directionforourtimes.org. We encourage everyone to print and distribute these booklets.

Other books by Anne, a lay apostle

Climbing the Mountain
Discovering your path to holiness
Anne's experiences of Heaven

The Mist of Mercy
Spiritual Warfare
Anne's experiences of Purgatory

Serving In Clarity
A Guide for Lay Apostles
of Jesus Christ the Returning King

In Defense of Obedience
and
Reflections on the Priesthood
Two Essays on topics close to the Heart of Jesus

Lessons in Love
Moving Toward Divine Intimacy

Whispers from the Cross
Reclaiming the Church
Through Personal Holiness